WOMEN, CREATION, AND THE FALL

WOMEN, CREATION, AND THE FALL

Mary A. Kassian

CROSSWAY BOOKS • WESTCHESTER, ILLINOIS
A DIVISION OF GOOD NEWS PUBLISHERS

CONTENTS

85546

PREFACE

Christian ideology has contributed no little to the oppression of women.

Simone de Beauvoir

The penning of these words by Simone de Beauvoir marked the beginning of the era of women's liberation. Her questions about the role of women in secular society in the sixties became the topic of discussion for the religious community in the seventies. Since that time, a myriad of books and articles have been published on the *Biblical* role of women. Yet, much confusion remains.

This book reflects my own personal struggle in coming to grips with the Biblical role of women in contemporary society. My thoughts have crystallized in this form, for in my studies I have found the bulk of writings on the Biblical role of women irresponsible in their handling of the Bible. The ones sound in their exegesis were few and far between and often were so technical they made tedious reading. I have thus attempted to broach the subject responsibly, employing the literal (grammatical-historical) method of interpretation, and then to present my conclusions in a readable manner.

The topic of women's role and ministry is volatile. Though eager to deal with it, I fear misunderstanding and misapplication of what I say. Therefore, I need to lay out some basic premises for the book. First, the concepts presented apply specifically to the Christian community. They cannot be applied to society in general. People who have not experienced the Holy Spirit's regeneration are incapable of understanding or applying Biblical principles, for it is only through the power of God's Spirit within us that we are freed for obedience. Second, I believe the *spirit* or intent of our actions is just as important as our actions themselves. Following the Biblical model of the role of women without Christ-centered heart motivation produces only legalism. As far as I am concerned, rigidly applying Biblical teaching, while neglecting a spirit of freedom, unity, love, and understanding among believers, is a greater mistake than that of theological error.

In writing this book, I have attempted to present the Biblical ideal for the role of women. I understand that godly ideals and the practical outworking of correct doctrine are not always attainable in a sinful society, yet I feel that integrity in our obedience to Scripture must always be pursued. For in the role of women, as in any other area of life, only God's Word holds ultimate authority.

Finally, it is my pleasure to thank all those who have commented on various drafts of the manuscript. I am also deeply indebted to my parents for their faithful example; to Sheelagh, for her many prayers on my behalf; to Mike, for his unique perspective; to Sue, for her good questions; and most of all to Brent, for his constant love, support, and encouragement.

INTRODUCTION

Where does one begin to talk about the role of women? Emotions and sensitivities run high on this issue. Societal pressures and our own life experiences combine to make objectivity an elusive ideal. A myriad of conflicting views makes it difficult to reach a definite, viable conclusion as to what the role of the Christian woman should be.

The creation and Fall of mankind lay the foundation for New Testament role directives. We must, therefore, begin our study by turning to the early pages of Genesis to find God's original intent for woman.

Part One of this book will examine the created order in Eden, the distortion of this order by the Fall, and the implications for us today. Finally, it will discuss authority and submission inherent in the first male-female relationship and briefly overview hierarchical relationships in the New Testament.

Part Two will investigate God's order in the home by analyzing male and female roles in marriage and by discussing the problem of sex stereotyping.

Part Three examines God's order in the church. The most extensive section of this book, it deals with difficult passages and questions regarding headship and head coverings, the verbal participation of women in church meetings, and the appointment of women to church offices. Part Three will also investigate the feminist movement within the church, ministry, and common hindrances to women's ministry.

The role of women is a broad topic, overlapping many other areas of special concern. It is difficult to present it in isolation. I am acutely conscious of this fact, yet for pragmatic reasons I have had to strictly limit the parameters of this work. I only hope that the area chosen for study is adequate for a basic understanding of the created order and New Testament directives and that it answers at least some of the burning questions regarding the role of women today.

PART ONE:

GOD'S ORDER IN CREATION

ONE

THE CREATED ORDER

An understanding of creation is central to a correct understanding of male and female roles, as all Biblical teaching on roles is contingent on this historic event. Gender roles are rooted in the created order, and apart from this context, cannot be understood. Therefore the Genesis account of creation is the underpinning for New Testament teaching on the role of women.

> Then God said, "Let us make man in our image, in our likeness, and let them rule over the fish of the sea and the birds of the air, over the livestock, over all the earth, and over all the creatures that move along the ground."
>
> So God created man in his own image, in the image of God he created him; male and female he created them.
>
> God blessed them and said to them, "Be fruitful and increase in number; fill the earth and subdue it. Rule over the fish of the sea and the birds of the air and over every living creature that moves on the ground." (Genesis 1:26, 27)

> The Lord God formed man from the dust of the ground and breathed into his nostrils the breath of life, and the man became a living being.
>
> The Lord God took the man and put him in the Garden of Eden to work it and take care of it. And the Lord God commanded the man, "You are free to eat from any tree in the gar-

den; but you must not eat from the tree of the knowledge of good and evil, for when you eat of it you will surely die."

The Lord God said, "It is not good for the man to be alone. I will make a helper suitable for him."

Now the Lord God had formed out of the ground all the beasts of the field and all the birds of the air. He brought them to the man to see what he would name them; and whatever the man called each living creature, that was its name. So the man gave names to all the livestock, the birds of the air and all the beasts of the field.

But for Adam no suitable helper was found. So the Lord God caused the man to fall into a deep sleep; and while he was sleeping, he took one of the man's ribs and closed up the place with flesh. Then the Lord God made a woman from the rib he had taken out of the man, and he brought her to the man.

The man said, "This is now bone of my bones and flesh of my flesh; she shall be called 'woman,' for she was taken out of man."

For this reason a man will leave his father and mother and be united to his wife, and they will become one flesh.

The man and his wife were both naked, and they felt no shame. (Genesis 2:7, 15-25)[1]

In Eden, Adam and Eve lived in a world unmarred by the effects of sin. Their relationship was perfect and was characterized by unity and harmony. Here in the Genesis account of creation we see a prototype of the roles God had created for man and woman, and here we see the intended outworking of those roles. Although this passage is relatively brief, a careful analysis of it reveals much.

Genesis includes two accounts of the creation of mankind. Chapter 1 gives a summary of the entire act of creation, including the creation of male and female. Chapter 2 zeroes in on the events of the sixth day, detailing the creation of the sexes. The former pictures the creation of male and female as simultaneous, while the latter puts the creation of the sexes into a time-frame. The man was created first, and then the woman was created from the man's side to be a "suitable helper" for him.

Chapter 1 focuses on creation from a slightly different angle than chapter 2. Unfortunately, many have attended to one account and have excluded the other. Chapter 1 has been cited as teaching the absolute, unequivocal equality of the sexes, while chapter 2 has been used as rationalization for the inferiority of woman.[2] Neither of these extremes is correct. Chapters 1 and 2 complement each other, and the true picture of the created role of woman emerges only when both narratives are viewed together as a whole. Genesis 1 shows the uniqueness and equality of human beings, while chapter 2 balances the equality with role distinctions. These concepts are compatible. Equality and distinction coexist in the created roles of male and female. Let's examine these themes more closely.

MALE AND FEMALE — CREATED UNIQUE AND EQUAL

The creation of man and woman is unique, for it was the first time a "consultation" took place regarding creation. Instead of saying, "Let there be man," as He had before said, "Let there be light," or instead of simply commanding the earth to bring forth man, we see a divine deliberation. God said, "Let *us* make man in *our* image, in *our* likeness. . . ." Scripture represents God as conferring with the other persons of the Godhead before going ahead with man's creation. This in itself proclaims the distinction of humans from the rest of creation.

The second fact which markedly contrasts man and woman to the rest of creation is that they were made in the *image* and *likeness* of God. Although the precise meaning of the image of God is still being discussed, there is sufficient evidence to indicate that the image of God in human beings is reflected in their moral, intellectual, and spiritual likeness to Him[3] (Colossians 3:10; Ephesians 4:24; 1 Corinthians 11:7). Humans thus reflect the image of God by virtue of their spiritual natures. They possess unique intellectual capacity, unique moral potential, and a unique spiritual personality in which the image of God is indelibly printed.[4] Mernahem Kasher summarizes: "Man alone among living creatures is gifted, like his Creator, with moral freedom and will. He is capable of knowing and loving God, and of holding spiritual communion with Him; and man alone can guide his actions in accordance with reason."[5]

The image-likeness of God is a trait exclusively human. The Creator deliberated over the making of this unique species, and then gave them a unique blessing. Only humans were given the right and the command to multiply and subdue the earth. Humans are thus supreme over all else created. This status has not evolved through the process of natural selection, but existed from the very beginning. Therefore, according to Genesis 1, all human beings are unique in that they have been blessed with moral, intellectual, and spiritual likeness to God and that they have been placed in a position of authority over the animals.

Genesis 1 gives no indication of any difference between male and female. They are equal in their relationship to *God* (they are both created in His image) and to *nature* (they are both to fill the earth and subdue it).[6] Chapter 2 provides details of the creation of male and female and their relationship to *each other*. It supports and underlines the equality presented in chapter 1, yet shows created role differences between the two sexes.

CREATION OF THE MALE (Genesis 2:7-19)

In the time-frame narrative of Genesis 2, we see the creation of the male occurring prior to the creation of the female. This chronological fact cannot be ignored or trivialized, as the Apostle Paul used this as basis for the principle of headship (this concept will be dealt with at length later). Because the New Testament refers to the order of creation, the sequence in which male and female were created is significant.

After God created the male, He placed man in the garden of Eden to "work it and take care of it" (Genesis 2:15). Although the work Adam was to perform was not work as we now know it, his life was not one of indolence. He had WORK to do before the Fall. God gave Adam *responsibility* from the very beginning. God also gave Adam *authority*. He brought all the beasts of the field and all the birds of the air to Adam to be named. Whatever Adam decided to call the animals, that was their name.[7]

In the Semitic world, the naming of something or someone was a statement of lordship or authority.[8] Throughout Old Testament history, the chief officials of armies changed the names of people or territories they had conquered (Daniel 1:7; Numbers 32:38, 42; 2 Kings 23:34; 24:17). God named the light, the darkness, the firmament, the dry land, and the gathered waters to show His sovereign dominion over His creation. He called them Day, Night, Heavens, Earth, and Sea, respectively. Adam's naming of the animals demonstrates his sovereignty and authority over them.[9]

Although dominion over the earth was given to humans in general, only Adam, the male, was given the responsibility to tend the garden and the authority to name the animals. Woman had not yet been created. Again, this fact is important, as we shall see later.

CREATION OF THE FEMALE (Genesis 2:20-23)

As God created, He evaluated His own work. After creating light, separating the light from darkness, and creating sky, land and seas, God evaluated His work as "good." He then created vegetation, the sun, the moon, the stars, and all living creatures. This work was also judged to be good. "So God created man in his own image, in the image of God he created him; male and female he created them."[10] Following this creation of the sexes, God pronounced His final judgment on what He had created . . . it was all *very* good. Only one time during the days of creation did God evaluate the situation as "not good." This was prior to the creation of woman. Adam was alone in the garden. At this point, the Creator decided that it was not consistent with man's highest happiness to be alone. Even before God brought the animals to Adam for naming, God purposed to make a counterpart for him. Adam needed a suitable helper.

The Hebrew word for "helper" is a powerful one. It is usually used in a concrete sense to designate the assistant rather than the assistance given. Most other times when this particular word is used in the Old Testament, it refers to *God* being our helper.[11] It usually refers to divine aid or assistance.[12] To infer that the woman was to be a helper akin to God may be overstating the case. However, in the creation of female, we see that a doormat or servant-slave was certainly not what God had in mind. God intended to make a counterpart for the man, a vital helper for him, perhaps in much the same sense as God is a helper. More importantly, we can observe that the helper of man was made "suitable" — corresponding to, or like him, neither inferior nor superior. The woman corresponds to the man in that she, like him, is made in God's image.[13]

While Genesis 2 reemphasizes the essential equality of woman presented in chapter 1, it emphasizes that the creation of the female differed from the creation of the male. Francis Schaeffer noted that although the differences between the creation of male and female may seem trivial, they cannot be ignored without bringing real destruction to our theology. He observed that the Bible describes the creation of Eve as a *specific differentiation*, in its own way as much a differentiation as the creation of Adam himself.[14]

Eve was created in a different manner. She was created from the side of Adam rather than from the dust of the earth. She was also created for a different purpose. She was to be a suitable helper or counterpart to Adam. Adam and Eve were equal in terms of their standing before God, yet different from the very outset with regard to their purpose and function. The role differences and concurrent equality were understood by the first man and woman, and these are reflected in the interaction between the two.

ORIGINAL RELATIONSHIP BETWEEN MAN AND WOMAN

The primary focus of the relationship between the first man and woman was unity. When Adam saw the woman for the first time, he said, "This is now bone of my bones and flesh of my flesh; she shall be called 'woman,' for she was taken out of man." (Genesis 2:23). Adam recognized the female God had created as being part of himself, made out of the same substance. "Bone of my bones" means bone, body, self, self-same.[15] "Flesh of my flesh" emphasizes and amplifies the same idea. Adam recognized that the woman was the perfect counterpart to him. While she was an individual in her own right, she and Adam were meshed together in the totality of their beings. Adam expressed his joyous astonishment at the suitable helpmate. It might be paraphrased as: "Wow! This is actually part of me! This is an integral part of my being! I'm going to call her woman (Hebrew: *ishsha*) because she was taken out of man (Hebrew: *ish*)."

Adam recognized the unity between himself and the female.

However, he also recognized his God-given responsibility and authority by naming her. (Adam's act of naming the woman occurs again in Genesis 3:20 when he gives her the name "Eve" — mother of all living.) If the woman and man were meant to have identical roles, God would have named the woman, just as He had named the man. In giving Adam the responsibility to name the woman, a hierarchical relationship between Adam and the woman is established from the very outset. This in no way belittles the woman or assigns to her a lesser role. It simply reflects the difference between the roles that God had assigned to each. Adam was to be the leader in the relationship and the woman was to be the helpmate. These assigned roles blended together and coexisted alongside a perfect oneness and unity.

The name Adam gives the woman in Genesis 2:23 reemphasizes the primary characteristic of their relationship — unity. The Hebrew word for woman, *ishsha*, sounds like the Hebrew word for man, *ish*. While Adam could have called the woman anything he pleased, he recognized this creature as part of himself. Adam gave the woman her own name to recognize her uniqueness as an individual. He included his name within hers as a recognition of the unity between them.

The passage continues with: "For this reason a man will leave his father and mother and be united to his wife and they will become one flesh." It is not certain whether this was a statement of God at the time, or if it was added by Moses when Genesis was written. However, one thing is clear — because of the created order and unity between man and woman/husband and wife, a man will leave the close ties he has with his parents and will be united to his wife.

United means to cleave, cling, stick to, follow closely, join to, cling to someone in affection and loyalty.[16] "One flesh" reflects the totality of being: the heart, soul, and body united as one. This passage explicitly declares that the endearing marriage union is to be of a more intimate and sacred nature than any other relationship. The parties in a marriage relationship were to see themselves as entirely and indissolubly united, as if they were in reality one person, one soul, one body.[17]

To summarize, God's created order, His intended pattern, was one of unity. However, this order did not designate identical roles to

Adam and Eve. The leadership Adam provided was without chauvinism. The help Eve provided was akin to the help God Himself
provides. Adam gave loving guidance to the relationship without
domineering his wife. Eve willingly and gladly submitted to Adam's
leadership as his equal counterpart.

> In Eden . . . the man and woman knew each other as equals,
> both in the image of God, and thus each with a personal rela-
> tionship to God. Neither doubted the worth of the other nor of
> him/herself. Each was to perform his/her task in a different
> way, the man as the head and the woman as his helper. They
> operated as truly one flesh, one person.[18]

Genesis paints a beautiful picture of the intended roles of man
and woman. The hallmark of the first male-female relationship was
one of unity and equality expressed through complementary, distinctive roles. The created role relationship was one of delightful
perfection. Thus, after the creation of woman, we see God proclaiming His final evaluation of his creation. It was all good. It was all
very, *very* good!

TWO

BORN CURSED

In the garden, man and woman lived in a state of perfection. They experienced total harmony with the Creator, with His creation, and with each other. This balance was destroyed when woman and man submitted to the will of the tempter rather than to the will of God. At that point in time, both the woman and man were cursed, inalterably changing the course of history and the outworking of the original created order.

> Now the serpent was more crafty than any of the wild animals the Lord God had made. He said to the woman, "Did God really say, 'You must not eat from any tree in the garden'?"
>
> The woman said to the serpent, "We may eat fruit from the trees in the garden, but God did say, 'You must not eat fruit from the tree that is in the middle of the garden, and you must not touch it, or you will die.'"
>
> "You will not surely die," the serpent said to the woman. "For God knows that when you eat of it your eyes will be opened, and you will be like God, knowing good and evil."
>
> When the woman saw that the fruit of the tree was good for food and pleasing to the eye, and also desirable for gaining wisdom, she took some and ate it. She also gave some to her husband, who was with her, and he ate it. Then the eyes of both of them were opened, and they realized they were naked; so they sewed fig leaves together and made coverings for themselves.

Then the man and his wife heard the sound of the Lord God as he was walking in the garden in the cool of the day, and they hid from the Lord God among the trees of the garden. (Genesis 3:1-8)

THE TEMPTATION

Satan knew that both man and woman were created in the image of God. He knew that they were moral beings, created with the capacity to make decisions and to choose whether or not to obey. Why did the serpent tempt the woman rather than the man? Some expositors say that it is because the woman was weaker, inferior to the man. Had Satan first tempted the man, mankind would not have fallen. Others go to the opposite extreme.[1] They say that the serpent went to the woman first because she was the final perfecting element in creation. In causing the woman to fall, man was also destined to fall; but if the man fell first, the woman (the perfection) might not have disobeyed God's command. Another common explanation is that the tempter addressed the woman because she had not personally received the prohibition from God as Adam had.[2] Finally, a fourth possibility is that the serpent approached her because of a difference in woman's personality which made her more vulnerable to attack. Some of these explanations appear plausible, but we may never conclusively grasp the serpent's plan.

DOUBT AND DESIRE

The tempter's first words were, "Did God really say . . . ?" This was not a straightforward question. It was, rather, a deliberate distortion of a fact. "So God has *actually* said . . .?" perhaps captures the flavor of the Hebrew more accurately.[3] Satan was, in essence, jeering and scoffing at the word of God and planting seeds of doubt regarding the character of God in the woman's mind.

The tempter makes a massive affirmation, adopting a tone of surprise and indignation or else of feigned compassion, because he wishes to make the fact seem *outrageous*. Playing craftily on the denial, "You shall not eat of any tree of the garden," he presents the ban as a monstrous deprivation. It is not so much God's word on which he casts doubt as his *goodness*.[4]

First, the serpent casts doubt on the character of God, depicting Him by implication as selfish, jealous, oppressive, and repressive.[5] Second, the serpent points to the material, aesthetic, and mental enrichment which the fruit offers. "The woman saw that the fruit of the tree was good for food and pleasing to the eye, and also desirable for gaining wisdom. . . ."

Thus, the temptation can be summarized as planting doubt and appealing to desire. The serpent cast doubt in the woman's mind regarding the character of God and appealed to the woman's desire for the good and admirable.

THE FALL

". . . she took some and ate it. She also gave some to her husband, who was with her, and he ate it." Although the dialogue of chapter 3 is between the serpent and the woman, Adam is obviously present. The woman was the first to eat the fruit and break God's command. Scripture informs us that the woman was *deceived* in taking the fruit. The man took the fruit after the woman, and he was *not* deceived.[6] The woman was tricked into disobedience, while Adam took the fruit knowingly, going against the explicit command of the Creator.

The results of sin were instant. The created order had been violated, impairing the couple's relationship to God as well as their relationship to each other.[7] Adam and the woman lost the fundamental sense of oneness they had before the Fall. Before sinning, the woman talks about their mutual actions in the first person plural: "We may eat." After sinning, Adam and the woman employ only the singular: "I heard," "I feared," "I was naked," "I hid." Their unity had disintegrated.[8] This fact is further reflected in the "opening of their eyes" to realize they were *naked*.

The Hebrew word for "naked" is derived from the word which means to be exposed or laid bare.[9] Prior to sinning, the couple was totally oblivious to their naked state. Their lack of embarrassment suggests an innocence. After disobeying God's command, they became painfully aware of their guilt — stripped, as it were, of the perfection they were once clothed in. They felt guilt, fear, and spiritual nakedness before God. So much so that when the Lord God came to the garden in the cool of the evening, Adam and Eve hid themselves from His presence.

It is significant that when God confronted Adam and Eve, He asked both for explanations as to their behavior. Both were treated as responsible beings; both were held accountable for their actions. Adam, when questioned, shifted the blame onto the woman rather than acknowledge his own guilt. Eve likewise did not accept responsibility for her actions, but accused the serpent for her deception. God did not give the serpent a chance to explain. Instead, He cursed the serpent and revealed his eventual defeat.[10] God then proclaimed the judgment on man's and woman's disobedience.

THE CURSES

The sentences passed on man and woman affected their relationship to God, nature, and each other. These judgments affected Adam and Eve after the Fall and have affected every human being since. Here in Genesis the battle between the sexes begins.

The Curse on Woman

> To the woman he [God] said, "I will greatly increase your pains in childbearing; with pain you will give birth to children. Your desire will be for your husband, and he will rule over you." (Genesis 3:16)

The curse on women is twofold — pain in childbearing and confrontation in the male-female relationship. The word "pains" comes from the Hebrew word meaning pain, sorrow, and toil. The root of this word refers to physical pain as well as emotional sorrow.[11] Other similar Hebrew words have the connotations "to writhe," "to grieve," "to become tired, weary," "to be irritated," "angry," and "to be bitter, despairing."[12] The Hebrew word for "childbearing" refers to the birth process, while the word for giving birth may describe the act of a woman giving birth to a child, or in a broader sense, the whole procedure involved in producing or raising a child.[13]

Childbirth is painful. I had read about it and believed it before the birth of my first child, yet nothing could have prepared me for the intense agony of labor. Labor pain is simply inexplicable to one who has not experienced it. Dr. Ronald Melzack, a leading expert in the field of pain, has recently completed research on the intensity of labor pain. He found that, on average, labor pain ranks among the severest. According to his study, it may be exceeded only by the suffering of some terminal cancer patients and often is worse than having a finger amputated without anesthetic.[14] It is difficult to imagine a relatively pain-free birth process; however, this is what the Creator had in mind prior to the Fall. Thus, the first part of the judgment on woman decreed physical and mental pain as well as emotional grief and turmoil in childbearing.

The second part of the judgment on woman is just as significant; yet it is often overlooked. Few are aware of its implications. "Your desire will be for your husband, and he will rule over you."

Some have interpreted this pronouncement to mean that woman would find man sexually or psychologically desirable. Others have interpreted the clause to mean that the woman would desire only what the man desires, and that she would have no command over herself.[15] However, I believe a third interpretation more naturally arises from the Hebrew words and sentence structure. I consider it the closest to the Biblical author's intent and the best explanation for the role difficulty women experience to this day.

First, let us define the key words:

desire — attract, impel, longing, of desire or affection: intense drive, longing of woman for man, of man for woman, of beast to devour; hungering, intent upon.[16]

rule — to have dominion, reign, rule; to master.[17]

Although these definitions shed some light on the intended meaning, we cannot conclusively determine the author's intent in this manner. We must also consider the immediate context, the literary structure of the sentence, and the use of the words elsewhere.[18]

In the immediate context, God is judging sin. Therefore, the "desire" of woman would not be something positive. The pattern established prior to the Fall was a hierarchy of roles characterized by unity and oneness. The judgment would work against, rather than contribute to, this original created order and unity. The "desire" of the woman would work against the leadership of the husband, against God's original intent in marriage. Her desire would not contribute to his rule in any way.[19]

The literary structure of the clause supports this position. Literally, the clause reads: "You will do something to him and/or he will do something to you." This clause is actually a form of poetry. One-third of the Old Testament is written in poetic form. Hebrew poetry is characterized by parallelism, a feature which often helps shed light on the meaning of words in question.[20]

Three types of parallelism are used in Old Testament writings: synonymous parallelism in which the same idea is stated in different phrases, antithetic parallelism in which the idea in the first part is clarified in the second part by contrast, and synthetic parallelism in which the second part develops the idea presented in the first part.[21]

The clause we are studying employs antithetic parallelism. The second part, "he shall rule over you," is in direct contrast to the first part, "your desire shall be for your husband." The contrast of the second part of the clause unlocks the meaning of the first part. We can conclude, therefore, from the type of Hebrew poetry used, that a woman's desire is in direct opposition to the husband's rule. The words *desire* and *rule* stand as antonyms to one another.

The third important factor for determining the author's intent is the usage of the key word(s) elsewhere. The particular Hebrew word translated "desire" in this passage is used only three times in the Old Testament — twice by the author of Genesis (Genesis 3:16; 4:7) and once by another author (Song of Solomon 7:10). Examination of the way the Genesis author used the word elsewhere completes the picture of what he meant by woman's desire, and consequently what he meant by man's rule.

In Genesis 4:7, God is talking to Cain:

> If you do what is right, will you not be accepted? But if you do not do what is right, sin is crouching at your door; *it desires to have you, but you must master it.* (italics mine)

The similarities between Genesis 3:16 and Genesis 4:7 are striking. Again, we see antithetic parallelism: "It desires to have you and/but you must master (or rule over) it." Also notable, the Hebrew words translated "desire" and "rule" in Genesis 3:16 are *identical* to the words translated "desire" and "master" in Genesis 4:7. Since these verses were penned by the same author, it is probable that he used identical words and sentence structures to depict similar patterns of interaction. Thus, the curse on woman is that she would desire to conquer/devour/have her husband in the same way sin desired to have Cain. At the same time, the husband would attempt to rule/have dominion/reign over his wife in the same way Cain was to rule over sin.

To summarize, the best interpretation of the desire-rule clause is that after the Fall, women would rebel against their designated role and that men would abuse their role of leadership, thus creating tension in the male-female relationship.

The Curse on the Man

> To Adam he [God] said, "Because you listened to your wife and ate from the tree about which I commanded you, 'You must not eat of it,' Cursed is the ground because of you; through painful toil you will eat of it all the days of your life. It will produce thorns and thistles for you, and you will eat the plants of the field. By the sweat of your brow you will eat your food until you return to the ground, since from it you were taken; for dust you are and to dust you will return."

The curse on Adam was twofold as well. First, God cursed the ground. Nature would no longer be in subjection to Adam. The earth would no longer spontaneously yield the fruits required for man's existence. The man would be obliged to gain the necessaries of life by strenuous exertion. Simple labor in the tillage of the earth was not a part of the curse, but was the destiny of man from the start. It was laboring in toil and sorrow, exhausting and wearing out the physical energies by the hardships of the fields, that made Adam's judgment so bitter. His labor otherwise would have been a mere pleasant recreation.[22]

The second part of Adam's curse reflects the judgment God passed on the entrance of sin into the world. Adam had been given authority and responsibility in the first male-female relationship. Because Adam didn't intervene during the deception of the woman, and because he followed her deception with his own willful disobedience, *Adam*, not Eve, is held responsible for sin entering the world.[23] Adam was ultimately held responsible for the violation of God's command. In God's eyes, he was *more* guilty than Eve. The corresponding penalty was death and corruption, both physical and spiritual.[24] This sentence is the most far-reaching. It included the woman and all of mankind. Prior to the Fall, man was destined to live forever spiritually and physically. Therefore, through Adam, the whole human race has come under the curse of physical death and corruption. All of mankind stands spiritually condemned as lost sinners because of Adam.

THE CREATED ORDER BROKEN

Evil is not in the good that God has created, but in the rejection of the order that God has instituted for the enjoyment of the world.[25]

It has been suggested that the sins of woman and man were not all that bad. "Eve had the right idea," some claim. "Surrounded in Eden by an infinitely varied, deliciously fascinating environment, she rejected the haven of blissful ignorance and reached for knowledge — of herself and the world around her."[26] And who can fault Adam for supporting his wife in this quest?

No. The sin of woman and man was not that they desired knowledge, but that they misused and violated God's created order. Blocher observes that it is always in his use of the created order that man exercises the autonomy he pretends to have seized. For whenever man decides to be like God, "knowing good and evil," he rejects the created order and fails lamentably. The consequence of this offense was a continuing rebellion against this very order by all creation — humans, animals, nature, and the earth.

Eve broke God's order for the sake of earthly enjoyment, pleasure, and knowledge. She was punished, first with the sorrows and

pains of pregnancy and childbearing, and second with an internal
rebellion against her role and a reciprocal harsh, domineering spirit
in the man (who had once exercised his role in gentleness and love).
In submitting to Eve's wishes and disregarding God's command,
Adam broke the line of authority God had established.

The judgments passed at the Fall may seem harsh; however,
God is perfectly holy and just. He had no choice but to pass judgment on the breaking of His command. In reality, the sentences
passed reflect both God's justice and mercy. Justice was shown in
the cursing of the serpent and in the punishment of mankind with
marred relationships, labor, and mortality. Mercy was shown in the
promise of eventual triumph over the serpent — the triumph of
Jesus Christ who would have the power to overcome the curse
imposed on mankind.

IMPLICATIONS FOR TODAY

The entrance of sin into the world changed man and woman's relationship to God, to creation, and to her/his fellow human beings. No
longer do women and men walk in harmony with God. The unity
and equality present in the first relationship has disintegrated. Role
confusion, rebellion, and disharmony reign. Hard labor, sin, corruption, and death are unmistakable realities that face us every day. The
judgments passed on Adam and Eve influence every human who
has ever walked the face of this earth.

Of specific importance to the role of women is the judgment
found in Genesis 3:16. This pronouncement sowed the first seeds of
male chauvinism and women's liberation. The hierarchy, which
functioned so well to produce unity and harmony prior to the Fall,
was subjected to abuse from both sexes. Women, from the time of
Eve on, would be born with a sin nature which would cause them to
fight against male authority. Men would be harsh, domineering, and
unloving in their attempts to crush and conquer women. Male chauvinism and women's liberation are nothing new. Genesis 3:16 is
where both originated.

The consequences of the Fall affect us today. Women experience pain and sorrow in childbearing. Historically, they have sought
to usurp male authority and leadership, only to be crushed and

oppressed. Men in turn, have abused their God-given role and have
been oppressive, domineering, unfair, and unloving. They have
often wrongly pronounced women inferior. The modern feminist
movement has risen in the past few decades to combat male chauvinism and domination. However, the principle of men ruling over
and women fighting back to overcome this rule cannot be broken by
our own efforts. This is not something that has evolved historically
and culturally. *It is a principle deeply engraved into our sin nature.*
It is a direct result of the Fall and the judgment of God.

God sent Christ into the world to destroy the power of the
curse.[27] At His second coming, the curses instituted at the Fall will
completely pass. Presently, however, we are still affected by the
kingdom of Satan. Women, specifically, are tempted to yield to mod-
ern-day philosophy regarding their role. Consequently, God has set
out clear principles and concepts in His Word to guide us in our
Christian walk. We have been given the examples and teaching of
Jesus and the early believers as well as apostolic example and teaching. Herein is instruction governing Christian conduct in personal
relationships, conduct in the Body of Christ, conduct in the assembly
of believers, and conduct in the world. New Testament teaching on
the role of women and men is given to counteract our natural sin tendencies. New Testament teaching on gender roles clearly instructs us
to willingly place ourselves back into the proper created order.

Women have been born cursed. Although many women would
wildly shake their heads in agreement and continue their plot to
overthrow male domination, they forget that the curse on women is
not rooted in the sin of man. The curse on women was brought
about by a woman. It does not consist of the subordination of
women, but rather in the *rebellion* against woman's subordination.
Women are cursed in that they rebel against the created order. It is
only when women embrace Christ and seek to live by the teaching
of His Word that they are released from the bondage of the curse. It
is only in adopting a Biblical perspective on male and female roles
that women will be alerted to the sin tendencies in and around them
and be truly liberated to fulfill their God-given role.

THREE

AUTHORITY AND SUBMISSION

Two basic concepts are inherent in the hierarchy of the created order — authority and submission. These concepts are not unique to the male/female relationship, yet they are repeatedly used in that context. A proper understanding of authority and submission is pivotal to our appreciation and application of New Testament teaching on the role of women.

The concepts of authority and submission are unpopular today. Our secular society has taught us to balk at the thought of hierarchical structure and the responsibility to submit. Individual rights are deemed more important than corporate responsibility, and any perceived intrusion on individual rights is vehemently contested.

The responsibility to submit in a hierarchy is often viewed as an intrusion on one's rights. This attitude has resulted in a breakdown of respect for authority and law. Parents, school teachers, law enforcers, government officials, and others in authority positions are openly mocked and defied. Hierarchy, and more specifically authority, is viewed as something to rebel against.

Because of the stigma attached to authority and submission within a hierarchy, it is important to begin by establishing the *Biblical* definition of these terms.

REINSTATING BIBLICAL HIERARCHY

Hierarchical structure is woven into God's overall design for creation. God is the source of the idea of authority, and He has allowed and ordained hierarchical relationships in which one party has authority over another.

> God is the source, not simply of all authority; He is the source of the very concept of authority (Romans 13:1). That the universe should be ordered around a series of over/under hierarchical relationships is His idea, a part of His original design.[1]

Scripture stresses the fact that each individual is equal and precious in God's eyes. It also reveals that God has established relationships within the framework of authority and submission. Equality in terms of spiritual privilege does not nullify the principles of authority and submission. Biblical equality and hierarchy are compatible concepts which occur simultaneously in Scripture.

The hierarchical structure which the Bible teaches can be represented diagrammatically as follows:

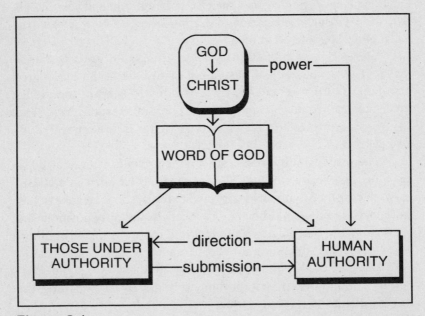

Figure 3.1

The diagram shows God in control of everything. Christ is equal to God the Father and yet at the same time is under God's ✓ authority.[2] God has given mankind His Word, and each individual is responsible for his/her response to it. Therefore, with regard to spiritual privilege, all people are equal. However, this equality exists within hierarchical relationships. God has ordained human authority structures and relationships in which one party is to lead and give direction while the other submits.

Some specific examples of hierarchical relationships present in the Bible are:

ROLE OF SUBMISSION	ROLE OF AUTHORITY
1. children	parents
2. slaves	masters
3. citizens	government
4. wives	husbands
5. believers	elders
6. Church	Christ
7. Christ	God

Although not all of the above relationships are ordained by God (for example: slavery), Scripture regulates the behavior of individuals within *all* of these hierarchical relationships.

Hierarchy is a part of God's plan for the ordering of His universe. God's principles of submission and authority apply to all. Let us therefore examine these principles in more detail.

THE PRINCIPLE OF SUBMISSION

Submission is the key concept to understand, for *everyone* is called upon to submit to God (James 4:7-10; Hebrews 12:9), and *all* at one time or another must submit to human authority. Believers who cannot submit to human authority do not know how to submit to God, for it is God who demands submission within human relationships. Conversely, believers will be ineffective leaders, incapable of properly fulfilling human authority roles, until they learn to submit to others. Submission is for *everyone*.

In order to understand Biblical submission, we must define it and deal with common misconceptions about it.

A dictionary defines submission as yielding to the power, control, or authority of another; being obedient and humble, willingly obeying another.[3] The Biblical meaning of submission is similar. The New Testament Greek word translated as submission or subordination is *hypotassō*. The root meaning of *tassō* and its various forms is "put in order," "arrange," or "put in place."[4] In its active uses, the word means "to make subject." In passive or reflexive uses, it means "to submit oneself." Each of the more than forty New Testament uses of the verb carries an overtone of authority and subjection or submission to that authority.[5] Thus, submission, simply defined, is obedience to one in authority.

Many misconceptions surround the idea of submission. People often confuse submission with a doormat or step-on-me-please attitude. Many maintain that submission negates human equality and that it demands a blind, mindless suppression of all reason. Let's consider each of these misperceptions in turn.

Submission implies inferiority.

The most common misconception about submission is that it implies inferiority. However, this is not true. In the business world, for example, authority and submission are well understood and seldom questioned. Workers submit to supervisors; supervisors submit to managers; managers submit to vice-presidents; vice-presidents submit to presidents. Almost everyone is, at one time or another, in a submissive role. And the role of submission does not imply inferior worth, but simply a *difference* in the position held.

Nor does the leadership role imply superiority, for value of the individual is not determined by the position the person occupies. Submission is not a matter of lowering one's worth, but of *recognizing the authority structure*.

To summarize, equality of persons and hierarchy are totally compatible concepts. Submission does *not* imply inferiority. It is a proper response to established authority.

Submission is blind obedience.

A second misconception is that the submissive person is docile and must blindly obey every whim of those in authority. The person who submits is pictured as a clinging-vine, with a dependent, passive personality. This individual buries his or her talents and intellect to subordinate all personal interests to the one in authority.[6] Some contemporary authors have identified submission as a self-retiring and self-effacing practice which denies one's gifts and quenches one's potential.[7] Although this picture of submission is deficient, some accept it as truth and utilize it to justify rebellion against authority.

Submission is *not* self-retiring and self-effacing behavior, nor is it blindly yielding to every whim of those in authority. Submission is an *intelligent choice*, and it is an *act of the will.*

Let us again reflect on the business illustration. The submissive worker need not be a mindless "yes man." He can and should try to maximize his potential. The worker can offer ideas and suggestions, develop new concepts, demonstrate initiative, and take on responsibility. If the supervisor makes a decision with which the worker disagrees, he can appeal the decision with wisdom and sound reason. Submission only comes into the picture when the supervisor dismisses the appeal and/or refuses to compromise. It is then the worker's responsibility to willingly submit to the decision. Indeed, this submission is considered the mark of a *good* worker.

Similarly, *all* those in positions of submission are to be responsible in developing their gifts, maximizing their potential, taking initiative, offering new ideas, and communicating their feelings. Obedience is demanded only if a conflict of opinion arises and cannot be solved though discussion and compromise. In this case, the one in authority is to make the final decision, and it is the responsibility of the one under authority to submit.

Submission is mere compliance.

A third misconception is that submission merely requires that one comply with the decisions of the authority. However, submission is much more than that. It is an *inward attitude* characterized by humility. It is an attitude by which we voluntarily and gladly obey those in authority over us. We obey *not* because they are wiser or better; our obedience stems from a recognition of their position of authority and from an inward humility which submits to that authority. Outward compliance without inward compliance is not submission. Submission is an *attitude* of the heart.

The one in authority is also required to submit.

Mutual submission is also an incorrect concept, for submission is the responsibility of the *one under authority*. Although admonitions to bend to meet the needs of a submissive partner in a relationship, as well as to lead with love, consideration, and respect, *are* present throughout Scripture, the one in authority is *never* asked to submit to the subordinate.[8] The term mutual submission is thus a misnomer and is foreign to Scripture.

Ephesians 5:21 is used as the prooftext to support the mutual submission concept. *Hypotasso* (Greek for "submit") in verse 21 is interpreted to mean submitting to the needs of *each other*. Mutually looking out for each other's needs and altering one's behavior for the sake of the other is in line with Christ's pattern of self-sacrificing love and is indeed what He wishes us to do. However, interpreting *hypotasso* as requiring *reciprocal* obedience within a hierarchical relationship obviously overlooks its New Testament meaning.

Hypotasso always requires *one* party in a relationship to submit to the other, and *not* vice versa. The context of Ephesians 5:21 supports this position. In this verse, Paul makes a *general* call to all Christians to submit to one another in whatever hierarchical relationships *they are involved in*. He then gives three *specific* examples of relationships in which submission of one party is required. Verse 21 is thus properly understood as an introductory verse to those which follow. As James Hurley points out:

> Verse 21, "submit yourselves to one another out of respect for Christ," is thus to be understood as a general heading indicating that there will be various situations in which certain believers will have to yield to the authority of others. The following text (5:22–6:9) sets out three particular relations in which this will be the case: wives will need to submit themselves to husbands; children will need to obey their parents, and slaves their masters. The idea of mutual submission has to do with various members of the congregation rather than with the two partners of each pair.[9]

Although the Bible does not teach mutual submission within an authority structure, it *does* teach principles of conduct which are to be mutually practiced by all believers. Believers are to encourage, edify, be devoted to, and live in harmony with each other. They are to exhibit Christlike traits of gentleness, patience, and kindness. Believers have mutual responsibility to show concern, love, and respect for each other, and to esteem each other better than themselves. They are warned against being conceited and against biting, devouring, consuming, provoking, envying, hating, and begrudging one another.[10] *This* is the mutual responsibility of both the one in authority and the one under authority. But *submission*, or obedience, is required *only* of the one who is under authority, not of the one in an authoritative or leadership position.

The one in authority is entitled to demand submission.

Those in leadership positions often feel that submission is their "right." However, in human hierarchical relationships, submission is not to be demanded. Rather the one who is to submit has the responsibility to do so because of his/her relation to Christ.

God's design calls for *willing* submission. This pattern is clear whenever persons are called upon to be subordinate. Those in human leadership positions are never told to *make* those under them submit. Submission for the love of Christ is set solely before the one who is to submit.[11]

Submission has limits.

Obeying those in authority over us is an intelligent act of the will. We are to submit to leadership just as we would submit to Christ himself. However, many people focus on the *limits* to the Christian's submission to human authority. They argue that our submission is first and foremost to God and that any authority which contradicts Biblical teaching need not be heeded. Thus, submission is often glibly dismissed as inapplicable when it becomes inconvenient or difficult or when it is perceived by the one under authority to violate one of God's principles.

However, the Bible does not qualify the extent of our submission to authority. If we find ourselves in a situation where obedience to authority directly contradicts God's Word, we should appeal to that authority. If our appeal fails, we must appeal to God Himself, for He is the one who has allowed us to be in a submissive position. Guidance in such specific instances must come from God Himself.

Consider the Apostle Peter. Frequently he was commanded by governmental authorities to stop preaching the gospel (Acts 5:28). Peter was unable to do so since his directions to preach the gospel had come directly from God. Even though he could not obey the government's wishes, his attitude of submission was evident. He willingly (never complaining or criticizing) suffered the consequences of his disobedience to them (Acts 5:41).

Practically, there may be situations in which submission to authority is limited. However, these situations are few and far between. Our focus should be on humility and obedience to authority in *all* circumstances. Submission may indeed have limits, but these limits are the exception rather than the rule. Obedience to God generally means obedience to those in authority over us.

To summarize, submission is obedience to one(s) in authority. It does not imply superiority or inferiority, nor does it negate the principle of human equality. Submission is a proper response to established authority. It is an intelligent choice of the will and an attitude of the heart. Submission is required only of the one under authority and is to be given willingly, motivated by love and obedience to Christ. The one in authority does not have the right to demand submission. Obedience to human authority is obedience to God.

THE PRINCIPLE OF AUTHORITY

The principle of submission does not stand in isolation from the principle of authority. Most dictionaries define *authority* as the right to command or act. In the New Testament, use of the word refers to delegated power, permission, or license.[12] Biblical authority is not taken upon oneself, but rather is given or delegated by another. For example, Christ was given authority by God; Christ gave the disciples and apostles authority; Saul was given authority by the chief priests, and the centurion was given authority by those above him.[13] Biblical authority is thus power and permission to command, act, or lead, which has been *delegated* to the one in authority.

Many people, feminists in particular, feel that the concept of authority is incompatible with other Biblical teaching. They argue that "no person can remain unspoiled by the corrupting effect of power when he is told that he holds by divine right a position of superiority in which others are duty-bound to subject themselves to him."[14] According to their reasoning, female subordination to male authority in the marriage relationship creates in the male the desire to dominate, exploit, and manipulate the woman as an autocrat lords it over his subjects.[15] On this basis feminists reject the teaching on authority and submission in hierarchical relationships.

Feminists' concern regarding corrupted power and oppression is valid. God has the same concern. He has commanded those in authority to exercise that authority with love, humility, and justice.[16] But New Testament writers *did not* eliminate hierarchical roles. Rather they regulated behavior within the roles to prevent abuse. As Litfin correctly states, "Wherever there is properly constituted authority, there is also the potential for abuse. The Biblical answer to this problem, however, is not to eliminate that authority, but to use it in a way that honors Christ."[17]

Jesus taught that authority was for the purpose of service (Luke 22:24-27). He warns against exercising authority excessively or arbitrarily in a "lord-it-over-them" attitude.[18] Jesus did not do away with authority. He was, however, concerned that authority be exercised in the proper manner. Those in authority have the responsibility to *serve* those under them. They are to be considerate and are to make leadership decisions in the best interests of those they lead.

Jesus did not argue against the disciples having authority; He simply regulated the *exercise* of that authority.[19] Although the tendency for any leader, affected by sin, is to be callous and overbearing and to disregard the person and feelings of the one under authority, the New Testament admonishes against this. Conversely, the tendency for the subordinate, affected by sin, is to be disrespectful and rebellious. The New Testament admonishes against this tendency as well.

For every human hierarchical relationship presented in the Bible, commands are given to both parties to counteract natural sinful tendencies. Those under authority are commanded to willingly submit, obey, and respect, while those in authority/leadership positions are to exercise their power with love and a serving spirit. Following is a list of God's bilateral commands:

COMMAND TO COUNTERACT POTENTIAL ABUSE

1. *Children* — obey.
(Col. 3:20; Eph. 6:1)

Parents — do not exasperate or embitter children.
(Col. 3:21; Eph. 6:4)

2. *Slaves* — obey, submit, serve wholeheartedly.
(Col. 3:22; Eph.6:6, 7;
1 Pet. 2:18; 1 Tim. 6:1)

Masters — treat slaves well, don't show partiality, provide what is right and fair, don't threaten them.
(Col. 4:1; Eph. 6:9)

3. *Citizens* — submit, obey.
(Rom. 13:1; 1 Pet. 2:13-19;
Titus 3:1)

Governing Authorities — God will regulate behavior of government.
(Rom. 13; Proverbs 21:1)

4. *Wives* — submit, obey, respect.
(Col. 3:18; 1 Pet. 3:1;
Eph. 5:22-24; Titus 2:5)

Husbands — be considerate, treat with respect, don't be harsh, love as Christ loved.
(1 Pet. 3:7; Col. 3:19;
Eph. 5:25-29)

5. *Believers* — submit, respect.
(Heb. 13:17; 1 Thess. 5:12;
1 Pet. 5:5)

Elders — don't "lord over" flock, be examples, lead by serving.
(1 Pet. 5:3-5)

An additional measure to minimize abuse of power is the command to *all* Christians to fulfill their mutual responsibility to love and serve each other. Hierarchical roles can and should exist within the framework of mutual love and service. The hierarchical structure cannot be dismissed as evil simply because of potential or real abuse. God has allowed and ordained hierarchical roles. The goal of New Testament teaching is not a society without authority/submission roles, but a social hierarchy, ordained by God and functioning in a manner that fulfills the teaching of Christ.[20]

THE EXAMPLE OF CHRIST

Christ is our example for the proper outworking of hierarchical roles. He is the *perfect* model both of willing submission and of loving authority.

The New Testament teaches that God the Father and Jesus Christ are equal — that they are one.[21] Yet, within the Godhead, a hierarchy of authority and submission exists. Christ is equal to God the Father, but is under the authority of God. The Bible teaches that Christ recognizes the authority structure and submits obediently to God's will. God is "head" over Christ; God is the one who delegates authority to Christ, and God is the one who put all under Christ's feet. Christ's position is thus one of submission.[22]

We are told that it was *God's* will that Jesus Christ die for mankind and that *God* is the one who sent Christ to earth. Christ, who was in very nature God, did not consider His equality with God something to be held on to. He made Himself nothing and obediently gave up His own life.

Christ's plea in Gethsemane is the epitome of submission. The night before His crucifixion, knowing full well what was about to transpire, Christ prayed: *"Yet not as I will, but as you will"* (Matthew 26:39). Christ did not want to die! If it had been up to Him, He would not have gone through with the crucifixion. Even though He had the power to stop it, Christ willingly emptied Himself of all His own rights and fulfilled His responsibility by yielding to His Father's will. He did not demand His rights although He was in His very nature God — equal to God. It is hard to imagine Christ saying to God, "God, I know You want me to do this, but as I'm not thrilled about the idea, I'm going to call down the angels and put a stop to this!" He could have, but He did not.

Submission is not an easy process. Pride and selfishness often get in the way. Although we as people are all equal, we are called to get rid of pride and selfishness and willingly submit to those in authority. Biblical submission involves following the example of Christ: *"Not as I will, but as You will."* This is how believers are to submit to God-ordained human authority.

The Bible tells us that God has delegated to Christ all authority. Christ could have called legions of angels to His side in an instant. He could have defied and destroyed all who resisted Him. However, Christ was humble. He did not come to be served, but to serve with love and humility (Matthew 20:28; Mark 10:45). Christ taught by words and example, and those in positions of authority should emulate His management of authority. Christ said to the apostles, "The greatest among you will be your servant" (Matthew

23:11). Therefore, Christ expected that the apostles would use their delegated authority for the purpose of serving others.

The qualities of servanthood, humility, and love do not nullify the principle or position of authority. Instead, they ensure that the authority will be exercised in the proper manner. Those in authority are to serve those who submit by loving and considering them. Also, they are to make wise leadership decisions for the benefit of those they lead. Authority exercised in a godly manner always protects those under authority from abuse. The primary motivation in the exercise of authority is love. Love demands the choosing of the highest good for those in submission.

Therefore, the New Testament revolutionizes the manner in which authority is to be carried out. Christ is an eloquent and eternal illustration that love (including service) and authority (hierarchy) are compatible.[23]

HIERARCHICAL RELATIONSHIPS REGULATED

The Apostle Paul regulated behavior within hierarchical relationships, but he did not intend to convey equal approval of them or to imply that they are all essentially of the same order.[24] The Scriptural principles of authority and submission tell us how to interpret the examples of hierarchical relationships given in the Bible. The examples, in turn, help clarify the principles, but the examples themselves do not necessarily have lasting applicability. For example, the principles of authority and submission are still valid, although the example of slavery does not apply in our country.

This is important to understand, for many feminists argue that if we accept Paul's teaching about wives submitting to husbands as universally applicable, then we must also accept slavery and government by kings as universally necessary.[25] They subsequently conclude that the examples are *all* culturally relative (i.e., that they do not apply to us today). The logical conclusion of the feminist line of reasoning would be that children need not submit to parents nor citizens to the government.

Feminists cite the Biblical example of slavery to discount all hierarchical relationships. However, the Biblical teaching on these relationships does not require one to accept slavery. Biblical *princi-*

ples are eternal, but *examples* of the principles may change, depending on the culture. We will review the examples of hierarchical relationships in order to determine which are of eternal significance and which were cited merely because of their evidence in the culture of the time.

Children/Parents

The relationship of children to parents was obviously established by God (Genesis 1; Proverbs 22:6). Children need leadership and guidance, and God has established parents as the authority to which children must submit. These roles are assigned by age and kinship.

Slaves/Masters

Nothing in the passages dealing with slaves and masters indicates that the relationship is ordained of God. Paul instructs men in the situation in which they find themselves without implying that God desires to perpetuate this situation.[26] Paul instructed slaves how to conduct themselves within the human institution, and yet at the same time he recognized that slavery could end. Slavery is not ordained by God, but behavior within this human institution was clearly regulated.

Citizens/Government

The Bible refers to government by king (1 Peter 2:13, 17), by Caesar (Matthew 22:21), and by "governing authorities" (Romans 13:1). Kings are mentioned only as an *example* of governing authorities. The New Testament does not require *kings*, but *does* present government as divinely instituted and gives instructions as to a Christian's response to it. Therefore, civil authority is ordained by God; however, the precise political form this authority should take is not specified.

Wives/Husbands

Marriage was ordained by God at creation. Certain roles were instituted at that time. The role of husband leading and wife submitting are reiterated and expounded in New Testament teaching. Therefore, this relationship has eternal significance. Marital authority is approved of by God, and roles are assigned by gender.

Believers/Elders

Christ established His Church universal and gave instructions through the apostles as to how the church local was to function. Believers in local assemblies are instructed to submit to the leadership of the elders. This relationship was established by Christ and is applicable cross-culturally. The role of elder is assigned by spiritual maturity and by gender.

Church/Christ

Christ established the Church. God obviously approves of the Church's submissive role.

Christ/God

Submission/authority roles within the Godhead are difficult to understand; however, Scripture is clear that Christ as God the Son submits to God the Father.

We can conclude that some examples of hierarchical relationships cited in the New Testament are temporal, and some are eternal. First, the parent-child relationship, marital relationship, and the relationship of believers to elders are *not* altered by time. Second, although behavior is regulated in the relationship of citizens to the governing authorities, the form of government may change. Finally, the institution of slavery is not applicable in contemporary Western society. If the apostles were alive today, they might have used the employer/employee relationship as an example of submission rather than slavery.

> . . . the unchanging word of God speaks authoritatively to the culture of man that God allows to pass away (slavery), to the culture of man that God allows man to appropriately change (civil government), and to the culture of man that God requires man to maintain (the form of authority and headship in marriage).[27]

The principles of authority and submission are still applicable today. They must be applied in those institutions which God has ordained.

SUMMARY

The principles of authority and submission are not popular in contemporary Western society. This unpopularity is mirrored in the
church. Contemporary theologians are attempting to disclaim the
hierarchical structure taught in the Bible, and many Christians have
been led to believe that the principles of authority and submission
are not applicable to us today.[28] Those who disown Biblical hierarchical relationships are considered "enlightened," while those who
adhere to the traditional interpretation are accused of "twisting" the
meaning of Scripture.[29]

My position is that hierarchy is taught by the Bible and that it
is *essential* to a Christian worldview. Christian men and women
need to learn how to fulfill roles of authority and submission in a
godly manner, for hierarchical relationships are part of God's plan
— part of His created order.

PART TWO:

GOD'S ORDER IN THE HOME

FOUR

THE INSTITUTION OF MARRIAGE

The phenomenon of single-parent families is becoming more and more prevalent in our society. A schoolteacher recently told me that over one-third of the students in his class live with only one parent. Although the majority of these single-parent families result from divorce, an ever-increasing number of people are single parents by choice. These are adults who want children, but who do not want to be involved in a marriage relationship. The exodus from traditional marriage is a growing trend.

The Biblical norm for the home runs contrary to this sociological trend. A husband-wife unit raising offspring is the ideal, be it in an extended or nuclear family. The bulk of Biblical teaching on male/female roles thus addresses these roles in the context of *marriage*.

While it is important for married couples to understand their respective roles, familiarity with marital roles should not be restricted to the married. Marital roles have ramifications which reach far beyond the home. For instance, the Bible's teaching on the functioning of the Church and Christ's relationship to the Church is illustrated by the marital relationship. The pattern for marriage is thus intricately woven into the order of the universe. Marital roles are foundational to what it means to be a male or female. It is vital that *all* Christians, both single and married, understand and uphold this God-ordained structure.

MARRIAGE — MORE THAN
A HUMAN INSTITUTION

The most recent statistics released by the province in which I live show that the divorce rate is 46 percent.[1] That means for every two couples getting married, one is getting divorced. This figure is even more astonishing since it does not reflect the couples who have separated or who are painfully enduring a bad marriage.

In contemporary society, marriage vows are taken lightly, and divorce is considered a good option. "As long as we both shall live" is being replaced with "as long as we both shall love." Increasingly lax divorce laws provide an easy way out of an unsatisfactory marriage relationship. It is no wonder then that some people shun marriage in favor of common-law, homosexual, or group relationships. What *is* a wonder is that marriage has survived at all and that it continues to be pursued by the majority of people as the utopian ideal. Why do people extricate themselves from one marriage relationship only to get involved in another? Why do most people still yearn for unity and oneness within a male-female relationship? The answer to these questions is not as illusive as some may think.

Marriage has survived because the desire for such a union is woven into our very being. The Creator ordained marriage in the beginning. *His* intention is that male and female yearn to be one. The permanent one-flesh relationship was *God's* idea, and God has placed the desire for this type of relationship within us. Although sin has distorted the perfection of marriage, we can still experience the good in it. When marriage operates the way God intended, we know a fulfillment, harmony, and joy beyond words — a small taste of the perfect unity which once was.

Marriage is good. It is good because it is God's idea. The institution of marriage has survived because it is much more than a human institution. It is an institution ordained and blessed by God Himself.

CHRIST'S VIEW OF MARRIAGE

Jesus approved of marriage. He taught that it is a binding, permanent relationship between a man and a woman. We see this clearly in Matthew 19:3-10 where an encounter between Jesus and the Pharisees over the issue of marriage and divorce is presented.

Some Pharisees came to him [Jesus] to test him. They asked, "Is it lawful for a man to divorce his wife for any and every reason?"

"Haven't you read," he replied, "that at the beginning the Creator 'made them male and female,' and said, 'For this reason a man will leave his father and mother and be united to his wife, and the two will become one flesh'? So they are no longer two, but one. Therefore what God has joined together, let man not separate."

"Why then," they asked, "did Moses command that a man give his wife a certificate of divorce and send her away?"

Jesus replied, "Moses permitted you to divorce your wives because your hearts were hard. But it was not this way from the beginning. I tell you that anyone who divorces his wife, except for marital unfaithfulness, and marries another woman commits adultery."

Divorce was an issue of long-standing debate among Jews, and the Pharisees were seeking to entice Jesus into committing Himself to one side of the debate. There were two schools of thought within rabbinical circles — the school of Shamai and the school of Hillel. These schools were divided as to the meaning of Moses' teaching on divorce in Deuteronomy 24:1.

The school of Hillel taught that a man may divorce his wife for any reason at all. Divorce was allowed if a woman "displeased" her husband in any way — even if it were in as simple a matter as spoiling his food. The school of Shamai was stricter, maintaining that a man could divorce his wife only for a "shameful thing" or "indecency." This would not include adultery, for adulteresses were stoned to death. A "shameful thing" was likely behavior or dress considered improper or seductive. Both sides agreed that Deuteronomy 24:1 authorized divorce; they simply disagreed as to the grounds.

Jesus' answer appeals to the original created order. He states that marriage is *permanent* and that man should *not* separate what God has joined. Both rabbinical schools of thought supposed that the division of this "one flesh" of marriage was permissible. Christ replies that Moses' concession of divorce was not God's original design, but a regulatory measure to deal with the result of sin. James Hurley observes that:

> Jesus responded by interpreting Moses in a fashion which over-turned *both* sides of the rabbinic debate. Moses did not com-mand divorce; he permitted it because of the hardness of your hearts. (vs.8) This carries the debate to yet a deeper level, for it implies that the act of divorce is not only against the created design, but an act of a hard-hearted, rebellious person: sin.[2]

Jesus' disciples were shocked at His stringent expectations. He taught that women and men are intended to live according to the original pattern of a *permanent* one-flesh relationship and that divorce is not an option for those within God's plan.[3] Marriage is a practical, vivid illustration of the relationship between Christ and the New Covenant Church. We must agree with Francis Schaeffer that:

> The Bible teaches that the marriage relationship is not just a human institution, but rather it is in fact a sacred mystery which, when honored, reveals something about the character of God himself. Thus we find the man-woman relationship of marriage is stressed throughout the Scriptures as a picture, an illustration, a type of the wonderful relationship between the individual and Christ, and between the Church and Christ.[4]

Christ is the husband; the Church is His bride (2 Corinthians 11:2; Revelation 19:7-9; 21:9). The relationship between husband and wife, and between Christ and the Church, are carefully inter-twined in Scripture. "The two ideas are so fused that it is almost impossible to separate them even with, as it were, an instrument as sharp as a surgeon's scalpel."[5]

Since the marital relationship has implications which reach far beyond the scope of a mere human institution, Biblical directives for it *cannot* be brushed off as culturally irrelevant. Marriage has its roots in creation, and the pattern for marriage instituted by God is independent of culture and time. To neglect Biblical guidelines for marriage is to tamper with the very heart of the gospel, for this rela-tionship mirrors the relationship of Christ to His Church. The gravity of such offense cannot be understated. Nothing less than total obedience to Biblical instructions for male-female roles in marriage is acceptable.

MARITAL ROLES

New Testament teachings regarding marital roles clearly point us back to the created order and to the roles of male and female prior to the Fall. Even though God created the first male and female as equals, He assigned to each a different role and function. Adam was to be the leader in the relationship, while Eve was to be the helper. The hierarchical roles, enacted in a sinless environment, blended together to produce a relationship characterized by oneness of heart, soul, and body. This oneness, perfect within a hierarchical relationship, was marred by the entrance of sin into the world. Sin corrupted both the willing submission of the wife and the loving headship of the husband. From the time of the Fall onward, the woman's desire has been to control her husband and to usurp his divinely appointed headship. Men, in turn, have sought to rule and dominate women. The rule of love founded in paradise has given way to struggle, tyranny, and domination.[6]

It is crucial to note that a hierarchical relationship between male and female was not a part of the curse. God's original design called for the male to be in a position of authority and the female to be in a position of submission. The curse is the painful *distortion* of that design.[7] Men and women are cursed in that they rebel against and/or abuse God's design.

Contemporary writers err when they say that male leadership and female submission in the marital relationship is a part of the curse. For example:

> To suggest that the curse upon man is lifted through the redemption offered in Christ, but that the curse upon woman (*i.e. that woman is to be submissive*) somehow remains (with the result that all women must forever be penalized because of Eve's transgression) seems to be a false and inconsistent theological assumption.[8] . . . theologically speaking, the death of Christ released humanity from the curse brought about by sin.

Woman is no longer to be subjugated under male headship. The mutual and complementary relationship that Adam and Eve enjoyed before the Fall may now be restored.[9]

Christ *has* provided a way for unity between male and female to be restored, but to assume that this is to be done through the abolition of hierarchical roles is "false and inconsistent." The New Testament role directives clearly point us back to the hierarchical relationship man and woman had before the Fall.

New Testament role directives stand in marked contrast to our natural sin inclinations. God wishes men and women to *willingly* place themselves back into His original created order. The goal of New Testament role directives is to explain how to implement God's order. The end result will again be male-female relationships characterized by unity, oneness, and equality.

HEADSHIP

Let us now consider the specific New Testament passages that direct us back to the created order.

Wives, submit to your husbands as to the Lord. For the husband is the head of the wife as Christ is the head of the church, his body, of which he is the Savior. *Now as the church submits to Christ, so also wives should submit to their husbands in everything.*

Husbands love your wives, just as Christ loved the church and gave himself up for her to make her holy, cleansing her by the washing with water through the word, and to present her to himself as a radiant church, without stain or wrinkle or any other blemish, but holy and blameless. In this same way, husbands ought to love their wives as their own bodies. He who loves his wife loves himself. After all, no one ever hated his own body, but he feeds and cares for it, just as Christ does the church — for we are members of his body. "For this reason a man will leave his father and mother and be united to his wife, and the two will become one flesh." This is a profound mystery — but I am talking about Christ and the

church. However, each one of you also must love his wife as
he loves himself, and the wife must respect her husband.
(Ephesians 5:22-33)

The authors who vehemently reject hierarchical relationships
between male and female interpret this passage to negate authority
and submission within marriage. They argue that *mutual submission*
has replaced traditional submission;[10,11] that the word *head* used in
verse 23 means source — not ruler or authority;[12,13] that the husband's directive to love negates the hierarchy;[14] and that teaching a
hierarchy within marriage is "unacceptable idolatry."[15] These arguments are at best grasping at straws. They are emotional attempts to
support a preconceived viewpoint. Since the concepts of mutual submission and hierarchy have been dealt with previously, the only area
that warrants further discussion is the meaning of the word *head*.

The New Testament Greek word *kephale* is translated head.
Traditionally, *kephale* has been thought to denote authority and
headship. Recently, many authors have proposed that *kephale* has
another meaning.

The general argument that many feminist authors employ in
the Ephesians passage (as well as 1 Corinthians 11) is that *head*
refers to source, not authority. They argue that Paul was not suggesting that the man is in authority over his wife, but rather that the man
was her source or united to her and that he should be especially concerned for her as he is for his own body. Although this is an interesting idea, there are several major difficulties in interpreting *head* in
this way.

So many contemporary authors have taken it for granted that
source was a commonly known or easily recognized sense of the
word *head* for the Greek-speaking readers of Paul's epistles that the
legitimacy of this interpretation is not even questioned. Three references are quoted as basis for this interpretation: a 1954 article by
Stephen Bedale, an entry in the Liddell-Scott lexicon for classical
Greek, and a fragment of a poem preserved from a very early date
in Greek literature — *Orphic Fragments 21a*.[16] Wayne Grudem, a
noted Greek scholar, examined the article by Stephen Bedale and
found it to be faulty in reasoning and factually unsupported.[17] In
addition, the entry in the Liddell-Scott lexicon had been misapplied

to persons when it actually referred to things (e.g., the head, or source, or origin of a river).[18] Finally, the reading of *kephale* cited in the *Orphic Fragments 21a* is obscure, and it does *not* substantiate source as an acceptable interpretation of *kephale*.[19] There is no evidence in the commonly cited references to justify interpreting *kephale* or *head* as source or origin.

In addition to studying the commonly cited references, Wayne Grudem surveyed 2,336 other instances of the word *kephale* used in Greek literature by thirty-six authors from the eighth century B.C. to the fourth century A.D. He did not discover *any* instances in which *kephale* had the meaning source or origin. His survey demonstrated that source or origin is not a legitimate meaning for *kephale*, and that the meaning ruler or authority over has sufficient attestation to establish it clearly as valid in Greek literature at the time of the New Testament. Indeed, the meaning ruler or authority over was a "well-established and recognizable meaning, and it is the meaning that best suits the New Testament texts that speak of the relationship between men and women by saying that the man is the 'head' of a woman and the husband is the 'head' of the wife."[20]

In both secular Greek and in the Greek Septuagint translation of the Old Testament, the word *kephale* was used with the connotation of leader or ruler. *Kephale* in Greek literature had an acceptable figurative meaning as first, prominent, or supreme.[21] We should not change or reduce the meaning of *kephale* today so that it means something different from what it did in Paul's day. Interpreting *kephale* as source or origin is errant and unjustified.

A second major difficulty in interpreting *head* as meaning source arises in applying this meaning to other passages. For instance, Paul often used head-body language to reflect the relationship of Christ to His Church (Ephesians 1:20-22). It is in the context of the relationship of the Church to Christ (in which the Church is *clearly* directed to submit to Christ — Ephesians 5:22, 23) where Paul uses marital imagery. The submission of the Church to Christ, and of the wife to her husband, is seen as a consequence of headship. If one strips the idea of authority from the marital relationship, one must also deny that Christ has authority over the Church, for the relation of the wife to the husband is to be a *pattern* of the relationship of the Church to Christ. As Hurley points out:

The language of headship, subjection and rule in Ephesians 1:20-23 is paralleled in 5:22-33. In each Christ's headship is responded to by subjection. This model provides the pattern for a wife's relation to her "head." Christ's actions as head provide the pattern for the husband. Christ's self-giving love is to be imitated by the husband who uses all his resources for her good. Ephesians 1:20-23 and 5:22-33 have in common the head/body relation, subjection to the head, and self-sacrificing rule for the sake of the body. Only with violence to the text can it be asserted that the idea of authority is absent from the language of headship and submission in Ephesians 5:22-33.[22]

Therefore, historical and New Testament usage of the word *kephale* as well as usage of the word in parallel passages thoroughly negates the head-as-source theory. Denial that the Ephesians passage supports authority/submission in marriage and in the relationship of the Church to Christ is simply misinterpretation. Even Jewett, an avid feminist, recognizes the only reasonable interpretation of Ephesians 5:22-33:

In this passage (Ephesians 5), the hierarchy of authority is drawn on a lesser canvas than in I Corinthians: Christ's subjection to God is not mentioned, and on the human plane express reference is made only to the subjection of the wife to the husband, not of the woman to the man as such. But the theological thrust is the same. In fact, within the limitations of the marriage bond, one can hardly conceive of a more clear and emphatic statement of hierarchy. Even the term used to describe the ideal relationship of a Christian husband to his wife is different from that used to describe the wife's relationship to her husband. While the husband is to love ($\alpha\gamma\alpha\pi\alpha\omega$) his wife, the wife is to fear ($\phi o\beta\acute{e}\omega$) her husband. This fear, to be sure, is not the cowering fear of a slave; it is rather the reverential respect which informs a woman's love for her husband as the authoritative head of the family. As the love which Christians have for the exalted Lord, the Head of the Church, is mingled with reverence (the fear of the Lord is the beginning of wisdom), so, by analogy, is the love of a wife for her husband who is her head. . . .[23]

The Ephesians passage is not the only one which supports the marital hierarchy. Colossians 3:18-19 admonishes wives to be in subjection to their husbands and husbands to love their wives; in 1 Timothy 2:11 women are told to learn in quietness with all subjection; in Titus 2:5 older women are instructed to teach younger women to be in subjection to their husbands so that the Word of God would not be blasphemed; and 1 Peter 3:1 urges wives to be in subjection to their husbands, even if the husbands are unbelievers.

New Testament passages thus intertwine to give us the overall picture of structured roles within marriage. The concept of the husband leading and the wife submitting within the marriage relationship is *not* based on isolated texts. The hierarchical structure in marriage is established to represent the relationship between the Church and Christ. Leadership and submission roles within marriage are compatible and necessary for a Christian perspective. Marriage, according to the Bible, has an irreversible authority structure which reflects the reality of God's created order.

FIVE

THE MALE ROLE IN MARRIAGE

Teaching on marital roles has often been lopsided. Many preach on woman's submission without allotting equal time to man's corresponding responsibilities. This is a source of endless frustration to women. They constantly hear how they are to submit, yet they seldom hear that this is tempered by the husband's responsibility to love.

As a result, some women have rebelled against Biblical teaching. As well, the overemphasis on the woman's role has led men to believe that it is their duty as spiritual leaders to help their wives learn submission. This belief fosters a harsh, domineering, and chauvinistic attitude that makes it even more difficult for women to fulfill their role. Much bitterness and rebellion could be avoided if the emphasis on marital roles were correctly placed on the male role of loving leadership rather than on the female role of submission.

My husband maintains that the climate of a marriage depends on the man. James Dobson shares this view:

> There is no substitute for the Biblical prescription for marriage, nor will its wisdom ever be replaced. A successful husband and wife relationship begins with the attitude of the man; he has been ordained by God as the head of the family, and the responsibility for its welfare rests upon his shoulders.[1]

Dr. Dobson's words reflect a depth of insight. If the emphasis shifted to the male role, Christian men would be urged to focus on how they could best love their wives. It is not cumbersome to submit to someone whose leadership is motivated by love and concern for those they lead.

LOVING LEADERSHIP

The male role in the marriage relationship can best summarized as one of loving leadership. This leadership is to be sacrificial and self-giving. It is exemplified by Christ's relationship to the Church:

> Husbands, love your wives, just as Christ loved the church and gave himself up for her to make her holy, cleansing her by the washing with water through the word, and to present her to himself as a radiant church, without stain or wrinkle or any other blemish, but holy and blameless. In this same way, husbands ought to love their wives as their own bodies. He who loves his wife loves himself. After all, no one ever hated his own body, but he feeds and cares for it, just as Christ does the church — for we are members of his body. "For this reason a man will leave his father and mother and be united to his wife, and the two will become one flesh." This is a profound mystery — but I am talking about Christ and the church. However, each one of you also must love his wife as he loves himself, and the wife must respect her husband. (Ephesians 5:25-33)

Loving is not an option for the Christian husband. Husbands are *commanded* to love their wives. Those who do not are sinning against God, for according to this passage, the leadership position of the husband carries with it an *obligation* to love his wife.

Loving leadership must involve respect for the wife. It also involves consideration for the highest good of the family in making decisions. Leadership (or headship) of the husband entails responsibility to act in love and to serve.[2]

Paul's words to the husbands in the Ephesians passage reveal that he was aware of a shortcoming in the way men executed authority. The men in Paul's time probably exercised it for personal satisfaction.[3] Paul calls them to consider what it means to imitate Christ. Jesus Christ gave Himself to meet the needs of the Church. Men are to do the same for their wives. Paul calls husbands to imitate Christ, not by setting aside authority, but by *serving* the needs of their wives.

Where there is authority, there is always potential for abuse, so the Bible gives special instructions to men. For instance, in Colossians 3:1, the command for husbands to love their wives is repeated with an additional directive not to be harsh. First Peter 3:7 directs husbands to be considerate and respectful to their wives, or run the risk of hindering their relationship with God:

> Husbands, in the same way be considerate as you live with your wives, and treat them with respect as the weaker partner and as heirs with you of the gracious gift of life, so that nothing will hinder your prayers.

Let us examine the verse more thoroughly. First, Paul directs husbands to follow Christ's example of love and sacrificial giving. Second, aware of the abuses of headship, Peter directed husbands to be considerate and treat wives with respect "as the weaker partner."

Many women resent this terminology. However, interpreting the phrase to mean that women are less intelligent or less morally capable than men is not supported by the context or by the rest of Scripture. Another opinion regarding this phrase is that weaker refers to a woman's relative physical weakness.[4] However, Peter was most likely referring to the "weaker" position wives hold with regard to authority. By marrying, a woman has accepted a position of submission that leaves her vulnerable and open to exploitation. Thus, Peter admonishes husbands not to take advantage of the wife's "weakness," or the wife's position of submission, by abusing their own position of authority.[5]

Finally, Peter stresses that women are *equal heirs* together with men of the "gift of life," or salvation. This mutual equality in the Lord gives balance and prevents misunderstanding on the part of men regarding the position given them.[6] Peter reminds men that women are *partners* together with them before God. For this reason men must be very careful *not* to abuse their position of authority. Men must listen carefully to their wives' point of view, consider, discuss, compromise where possible, and do everything in their capacity to achieve harmony. Peter's closing comment to believing husbands is a stern warning. Their relation to their wives will affect their relation to God.[7]

Godly leadership encourages those being led to fulfill their potential. It does not repress, exploit, or manipulate. It does not seek to be served, but to serve. Thus, the husband who loves his wife sacrificially, as Christ loves the Church, will listen carefully to his wife's opinion and consider her first in making decisions. He will trust her and delegate to her the decisions for which she has better perspective. In return, the wife is to love her husband, respect his opinion, consult him, and willingly submit if compromise cannot be reached. The husband's role and the wife's role blend together to create a oneness and harmony within the relationship.

The climate of the marital relationship does indeed begin with the man. If husbands were fulfilling their responsibility to love as Christ loved, women would have little difficulty submitting. In fact, submission to a loving husband would be a joy instead of a burden. It is imperative that men clearly understand and fulfill their role within the home. The lopsided presentation of marital roles which has long characterized Christian teaching must be rectified to place the primary emphasis on the husband's responsibility of loving, sacrificial leadership.

SIX

THE FEMALE ROLE IN MARRIAGE

Submission is the primary Biblical role assigned to Christian wives. Other New Testament instructions for wives include loving, fearing, and respecting their spouses. Although these directives are not easily followed, when both the wife and the husband are fulfilling their Biblical roles, unity and harmony reign.

Much of Biblical Christianity is a paradox. It is a paradox that we must lose our lives in order to gain them, and that we must give in order to receive. It is a paradox that fulfillment and joy for the Christian wife result from submitting to her husband. And by following Biblical role directives, the wife receives much more than if she were bitterly fighting for her "rights." Since this book is primarily aimed toward women, we will thoroughly examine the responsibilities of submitting, loving, fearing, and respecting.

SUBMISSION

Submission is not unique to the male-female marital relationship. This is a most crucial point. Marriage is only one example of a human relationship in which one party is to yield willingly to the authority of another. There is little difficulty thinking in terms of believers submitting to God, of believers submitting to the leaders of a local church, or even of citizens submitting to the governing

authorities. However, as soon as submission is applied specifically
to women within the marriage relationship, our natural, or perhaps
unnatural, reaction is one of rebellion, defiance, and disgust.

Submission to the twentieth-century woman is a dirty, archaic
word. But the meaning of submission has been twisted. Especially
within the context of marriage do the misconceptions exist. This is
not surprising. Women have a sin nature which causes them to balk
and rebel against male authority, and particularly that of their husbands. Furthermore, males have historically abused and domineered
women, harshly demanded submission as their right, and selfishly
exploited women to nurture their own egos. Both men and women
have sinned and contributed to the distortion of Biblical submis-
sion/authority roles. As a consequence, Christian wives and husbands need to gain a proper Biblical perspective of these roles.

Although submission has already been defined, we need to see
its meaning within the context of marriage. Therefore, let us again
address the common misconceptions with specific application to the
role of the Christian wife.

Misconceptions

The wife's submission implies the husband's superiority.
The idea of women's inferiority is contrary to Biblical teaching.
Superiority of *either* sex is nothing but a myth perpetuated by ignorance and sin. No movement has dignified the status of women more
than Christianity, and no single leader has uplifted women as much
as Jesus Christ. He showed deep respect for them. His views stand
in marked contrast to His Jewish contemporaries. For instance, the
rabbis would not teach the Torah (the Bible) to women, yet Jesus
delighted in having Mary sit at His feet to learn. He commended her
for having chosen "the better part," better than Martha busy with the
customary role of serving (Luke 10:38-42). Furthermore, Jesus'
male contemporaries often shunned women, yet Jesus and His disciples were accompanied on journeys by a group of women who
supported them financially (Luke 8:2, 3). Jesus showed courtesy and
respect for *all* women; even adulteresses and prostitutes were
treated as people of worth.

Women along with men received Jesus' compassion in His

healing ministry. In one such instance, Jesus called the woman He had healed a "daughter of Abraham," a title of honor which indicated her worth as a person and emphasized her equal spiritual status and privilege with the "sons of Abraham" (Luke 13:10-17). Jesus also frequently used women in His illustrations and parables (Matthew 21:31; 24:40, 41; Luke 13:19-21; 15:3-10; 18:1-14) and in His teaching about the kingdom of God. Women stood by Jesus at the cross, and they were given the great privilege of being the first witnesses of His resurrection. Men and women were included equally in God's plan for salvation and discipleship (Luke 12:51, 53; Mark 10:29-30). Women were held individually responsible for their response to the gospel. The coming of Christ and the kingdom of God presented an equality that was unprecedented.

The spiritual equality of women is evidenced in the epistles by the involvement of women in the early church as well as by the apostles' attitudes and teachings. Yet while the epistles teach the equality of male and female before God, they go beyond the teaching of the Gospels and present differences between male and female in role and function. Jesus did not specifically address the question of marital roles or woman's involvement in church government, whereas the apostles *did*. The apostles dealt with matters such as woman's submission in marriage, elders, deacons, and church functions. It is within these contexts that boundaries become most evident.

Feminists say that the apostles' teachings are *incongruent* with those of Jesus. They maintain that Jesus proclaimed total equality (identical roles), while the apostles perpetuated the discrimination taught by the rabbis.

The apostles are often labeled women haters. This is unfortunate, for their writings are inspired, authoritative, and harmonious with the teaching of the Gospels. The hierarchy of roles taught in the epistles is totally compatible with the equality of sexes taught throughout the New Testament. Duane Litfin rightly observes that: "Equality and difference of role are not mutually exclusive, but are indeed the two sides to the teaching of the word of God on the subject."[1]

The New Testament view of equality, equal worth and responsibility of the sexes within authority/submission roles, contrasts with the world's view. The world is striving for an equality which erases all boundaries of responsibility and allows people to do anything they please. Francis Schaeffer has called this "monolithic equality" — freedom without form.

> . . . the world spirit of our day would have us aspire to autonomous absolute freedom in the area of male and female relationships — to throw off all form and boundaries in these relationships and especially those boundaries taught in the Scriptures. Thus our age aspires not to Biblical equality and complementarity in expressing the image of God, but a monolithic equality which can best be described as equality without distinction.[2]

Schaeffer goes on to explain the tragic consequences of such thinking. To deny the Biblical pattern for male and female is to deny the character of God and His relationship to man. This denial is destructive and has consequences which affect all of society and human life:

> The idea of absolute, autonomous freedom flows into the idea of equality without distinction, which flows into the denial of what it truly means to be male and female, which flows into abortion and homosexuality, and the destruction of the home and family, and ultimately to the destruction of our culture.[3]

Equality of the sexes *is* taught in the Bible, but this equality is not monolithic. The Bible teaches that male and female are equal, but that they have different roles within the marriage relationship. In marriage, the wife's role is one of submission. Yet the submissive role, as conveyed in the epistles, is not one of passivity, but of voluntary action, of one equal to another.[4] Thus, the wife's role of submission is compatible with her essential equality to the male.

Submission is not unique to the woman's role within marriage and does not imply inferiority. Just as Jesus the Son is equal with and yet subordinate to God the Father, so a wife is equal with and yet subordinate to her husband. This has absolutely nothing to do with chauvinism, superiority, or inequality. Submission is *not* inferiority. It is the *proper* response to an established authority structure. Women are directed to *voluntarily* submit within the marriage relationship, for husbands are assigned the role of authority and wives the role of submission — *not* as a matter of their own qualifications, but rather, as a matter of divine appointment.

Submission requires the wife's blind obedience.

Submission does *not* mean that the wife must become a passive, mindless person who exists purely for the pleasure of her husband. The world tries to foist on us the image of a submissive person — a dependent, retiring, self-effacing, clinging-vine type who buries her own potential for the sake of another. However, this image is not at all the model the Bible presents.

Biblical submission is an intelligent choice. It is an act of the will. Women and men are equally responsible before God in developing their gifts and maximizing their potential, becoming all God wants them to be. Wives have a responsibility to express their opinions, desires, ideas, and to openly communicate their feelings. They, together with their husbands, must try to discuss, compromise, and agree on decisions. In the practical daily outworking of Christian marriage, conflict of opinion is usually solved through discussion and agreement. Superficially then, a functioning Christian marriage appears the same as the "equal" model of marriage which feminists are ardently striving for. There is, however, one major difference between the Biblical and the feminist model. In the Christian marriage, the husband is to fulfill the position of loving leadership, and the wife the position of willing submission. There is an implicit understanding on the part of the wife that if, after discussing an issue and expressing her view, her husband makes a decision with which she disagrees, it is her responsibility before God to choose to submit to her husband's decision. Submitting is the intelligent choice even if the decision made is not particularly intelligent.

Submission is mere compliance.

Some Christian women outwardly submit to their husbands, but inwardly rebel against their spouse's authority. These women may pretend submission to subtly win arguments and get their own way. "Well, all right, we'll do it *your* way!" is the common verbalization which conceals the thought, "I think you are wrong, but because I *have* to, I will obey you. You are *really* making me suffer by inflict-

ing your *stupid* point of view on my life." Oftentimes this false submission is followed up with statements such as, "I told you so!" or
"Remember when . . . ?!"

    Unwilling compliance is not Biblical submission. God looks at
the heart.

Submission is also required of the husband.

Mutual submission is a phrase which has been applied incorrectly.
Submission is only required of one party within any hierarchical relationship. The husband is *not* required to submit to or to obey his wife.
The husband *is* required to submit to God and obey *Him*. To do so, he
must encourage and edify his wife, look out for her best interests, be
devoted to her, be humble, gentle, patient, show concern and respect
for her, and above all, follow Christ's example of self-giving love for
her. The husband who loves his wife will try to please her and meet
her desires. Yet he is not required to *submit* to her. Wives who demand
that their husbands submit to them in half of the decisions are
demanding something contrary to God's Word. The Christian wife is
required to submit to her husband and not vice versa.

The wife's submission is the husband's right.

While our society emphasizes rights, the Bible emphasizes responsibility. The husband has no right to *demand* submission from his
wife. It is the *wife's* responsibility to willingly submit to her husband
in obedience to God. Conversely, the wife does not have the right to
demand love and respect from her husband. It is his responsibility to
love and respect her out of his obedience to God. Our focus should
not be "what about him/her?" but rather, "what about *me*?" As
Christians, we must learn to fulfill our own roles, trusting and
appealing to God for others to fulfill theirs.

The extent of the wife's submission is qualified.

Colossians 3:18 says that wives are to submit to their husbands "as
is fitting in the Lord." Some use this verse to justify women blindly
obeying their husbands in everything. Others interpret the passage
to mean that wives need submit only if the husbands are fulfilling
their responsibility. Neither interpretation is correct, for this verse
does not qualify the *extent* of a wife's submission. It simply reiter-

ates that submission to one's husband is the proper attitude for Christian women to adopt. For a Christian woman (one who is in the Lord), submission is the fitting or proper or right attitude. Scripture does not qualify the extent of a wife's submission. In fact, it even urges believing wives to submit to unbelieving husbands. In context, this implies that wives are to submit even if the one in authority abuses his position.

> Slaves, submit yourselves to your masters with all respect, not only to those who are good and considerate, but also to those who are harsh. For it is commendable if a man bears up under the pain of unjust suffering because he is conscious of God. But how is it to your credit if you receive a beating for doing wrong and endure it? But if you suffer for doing good and you endure it, this is commendable before God. To this you were called, because Christ suffered for you, leaving you an example, that you should follow in his steps.
> "He committed no sin, and no deceit was found in his mouth."
> When they hurled their insults at him, he did not retaliate; when he suffered, he made no threats. Instead, he entrusted himself to him who judges justly. He himself bore our sins in his body on the tree, so that we might die to sins and live for righteousness; by his wounds you have been healed. For you were like sheep going astray, but now you have returned to the Shepherd and Overseer of your souls.
> Wives, *in the same way* be submissive to your husbands. . . . (1 Peter 2:18–3:1, italics mine)

After addressing the issue of wives submitting, the passage discusses suffering for doing good. In context then, the matter of wives submitting is sandwiched between exhortations to do the right thing in difficult situations. This does not imply that a wife is meant to suffer, nor does it advocate remaining in a situation where constant physical abuse occurs. (In cases of abuse, the Biblical precedent appears to be fleeing or getting out of the situation.) Peter simply recognizes that submission is a difficult thing when those in authority are harsh or unjust. Andre Bustanoby observes:

Both Paul and Peter state the command to submit without qualifications. Peter's use of Sarah as an illustration of obedience is notable since Abraham *twice* in order to protect his own life, denied that Sarah was his wife and allowed her to be taken into a ruler's harem (Genesis 12:10-20; 20:1-18). The implication is not that a wife should allow her husband to sell her into prostitution if he wishes. But by stating the case absolutely, both Peter and Paul forestall capriciousness in the matter of submission.[5]

Since the Bible does not limit a wife's submission, it is unwise for us to do so. If a husband requests something which goes against God's Word, a wife must appeal to him with reason and sound judgment. If this fails, she must appeal to God Himself. If wives have consistently been applying principles of Christian conduct, this appeal to their husbands and to God will often solve the problem.

But should a wife obey her husband when, after all appeals, he orders her to do something she believes is wrong? Should she obey him and disobey God? There is no easy answer, for in most instances obedience to God means submission to one's husband — even if he is not a believer. Guidance must come from God Himself, and a Christian woman must prayerfully consider her decision.

For this reason I counsel single women to consider carefully the man they want to marry. "Has he the depth of Christian character that will not make unreasonable demands? Can you trust his spiritual judgment? Are you willing to submit yourself to him? Does he love sacrificially as Christ loved?"

Marriage is not to be entered into lightly or unadvisedly. To put it simply: If a woman has difficulty submitting to a particular man, she should not marry that man. God requests that Christian wives submit to their husbands, so one's willingness to submit should be dealt with prior to a marriage. If Christian women understood the directive to submit, I believe they would be more careful in choosing whom to marry. They would not settle for a man who does not have a deep commitment to God and to His Word. For in a truly Christian marriage, where both partners are committed to fulfilling their Biblical roles, submission is not at all oppressive. In fact, the husband's love and wife's submission liberate both parties from conflicts and free them to become everything they have the potential to be, as individuals and as a couple.

In summary, the role of submission does not imply the wife's inferiority, nor does it demand passive, blind obedience. Submission for the Christian wife is an intelligent act of the will. It involves an inward attitude which arises from a pure devotion to God. Submission is not required of the husband, but neither is the wife's submission the husband's right. Finally, Scripture does not qualify the extent of a wife's submission. Generally speaking, obedience to God involves submission to one's husband.

God's Plan for True Beauty

> Wives, in the same way be submissive to your husbands so that, if any of them do not believe the word, they may be won over without talk by the behavior of their wives, when they see the purity and reverence of your lives. Your beauty should not come from outward adornment, such as braided hair and the wearing of gold jewelry and fine clothes. Instead, it should be that of your inner self, the unfading beauty of a gentle and quiet spirit, which is of great worth in God's sight. For this is the way the holy women of the past who put their hope in God used to make themselves beautiful. They were submissive to their own husbands, like Sarah, who obeyed Abraham and called him her master. You are her daughters if you do what is right and do not give way to fear. (1 Peter 3:1-6)

Our North American culture places a great emphasis on external beauty. Our teeth, our hair, our skin, our clothes, our cars, and even our socks are supposed to generate sex appeal. Looking good is a number one priority, and the multimillion-dollar cosmetic and clothing industries reflect this fact. Although there is nothing wrong with physical beauty, our outward appearance should not become the focus of our attention. God looks deeper, and so should we. The 1 Peter passage describes the type of beauty women should strive for. Godly beauty comes from lives that are pure and reverent and from spirits that are quiet and gentle.

A life of purity involves more than absence of sin. It is a life wholly, unreservedly devoted to God. The pure heart is undivided. No hypocrisy or insincerity can be found there. The pure life focuses on one thing and one thing only — complete obedience to the Word of God. Reverence and purity of life go hand in hand. A reverent life respects God for who He is. A pure life responds to God in purpose and action.

Second, godly beauty stems from a quiet and gentle spirit within a woman. A quiet spirit does not refer to absence of speech, but to an inner tranquility. External circumstances cannot cause agitation or disturbance to the quiet spirit. A quiet and gentle spirit go hand in hand, for a gentle spirit is akin to meekness. A gentle spirit endures all things with an even temper. A gentle spirit is tender and free from proud self-sufficiency. Holy women in the past made themselves beautiful through leading pure and reverent lives, and maintaining quiet and gentle spirits.

Sarah is singled out as a vivacious example of beauty. The Old Testament tells us that she was physically beautiful, while the New Testament draws attention to her *inner* beauty.[6]

A brief character analysis of Sarah yields some interesting insights into her temperament. The accounts in Genesis reveal her as having a strong personality. Apparently high-spirited, she did not mince words in expressing her opinions. (For example: see Genesis 16:5; 21:10.) Sarah was not at all the dull, colorless, passive type we often associate with submissiveness. She was obviously strong-willed and opinionated, and yet the Bible singles *her* out as a model of submissiveness. A careful look at Sarah's relationship with her husband reveals why.

Abraham led and Sarah submitted. We are told in the 1 Peter 3 passage that Sarah called Abraham "master." She recognized the God-ordained hierarchy within their marital relationship. In the Old Testament and during the time of the patriarchs, "master" was a term of respect. Today the word carries the negative connotations of an oppressive master-slave relationship, but Abraham and Sarah enjoyed a bilateral relationship of love and mutual respect. In leading, Abraham evidently delegated authority to Sarah at times,[7] and at other times he made decisions based on her opinions and contrary to his own thoughts on the matter.[8] Thus, Sarah often modified Abraham's opinion. Although she willingly made decisions when authority was delegated to her, she never disobeyed Abraham nor rebelled against his authority. For the preceding reasons, the Apostle

Peter rightly identified Sarah as the role model of a submissive woman.

First Peter 3:1-6 also states that we are Sarah's daughters if we do what is right and *do not give in to fear*. Ungodly women are terrified of being repressed and unfulfilled. They fear submitting because they fear losing their rights. Christian women need not fear such things. Women who hope in God are free to do the right thing: submit to their husbands. The godly woman does not live as the world lives. Sarah is our example. And Sarah was *beautiful* — both outwardly and inwardly.

Outward beauty is attained by grooming and caring for one's physical features. Inward beauty, the lasting kind, is attained by carefully grooming and cultivating lives which are pure and reverent, spirits which are quiet and gentle. Godly character frees us to submit without fear of repression. Inwardly, we can be at peace, knowing that we will be fulfilled when we live according to *God's* plan. Submission is God's temporal plan for the Christian woman, and lasting beauty is the eternal reward.

LOVE

The second role directive for wives which is implied in the New Testament is that of love. Wives, unlike husbands, are never *specifically* commanded to love their spouses. In Titus 2:4, however, older women are admonished to *train* the younger women to love their husbands and children.

Three types of love are described in the New Testament. Although they are frequently used interchangeably, each has its own distinctive quality. *Philos* is the love of mankind, or brotherly love. *Eros* is erotic love which arises out of sexual attraction, and *agape* is love which is selfless and giving. Oddly enough, the instruction of Titus 2:4 is to "*philos* one's husband." Older Christian women are to train the younger Christian women to exercise a brotherly love towards their husbands. In other words, women are to demonstrate a love that promotes the well-being of their spouses.

FEAR AND RESPECT

Finally, Christian women are instructed to fear and respect their husbands. Fearing one's husband is NOT being *afraid* of him; it is a holy respect for his position of leadership, with the perspective that his position is God-ordained. As the Bible speaks of fearing God, women are to fear their husbands. This fear, to be sure, is not the cowering fear of a slave, but is rather a deep reverence, based on respect for the marital structure.

Respecting one's husband is similar in meaning to fearing him. To show respect for one's husband is to honor and esteem him, to show consideration or regard for him. Again, this is a response to the position God has placed him in. Respect is due, even though husbands may not always *deserve* it. The Christian wife gives respect out of obedience to God.

Failure to fear and respect one's husband undermines his ability and/or desire to lead. A woman fails here when she belittles her husband's ideas, nags him, mocks him, reminds him of his inadequacies and past failures, or criticizes him. A wife who sarcastically tears down her husband in front of others (even in fun), and who constantly resents her husband and draws attention to his faults, does not know how to obey this Biblical directive. An attitude of fear and respect leads to words and practical actions of courtesy and thoughtfulness. A woman who fears and respects her husband will always treat him as someone special.

In summary, the primary role for the Christian wife is submission to her husband. The Bible also advocates that love, fear, and respect be part of woman's marital role.

Scripture does not define the wife's role in marriage in terms of external tasks. Rather, the Bible gives directions for a wife's *inner attitudes*. In marriage, women are to submit to their husbands. They are also instructed to love, fear, and respect them. These attitudes will undoubtedly affect their behavior, but it is the *attitude* and *not* the behavior which is most important.

God desires Christian marriages to reflect what He originally intended for the relationship between a man and a woman. Because of this, Christian women are instructed to go against their natural sin tendencies to willingly place themselves back into the original created order of a marital hierarchy. Through God's Spirit, women are enabled to overcome the curse of the garden to once again willingly submit, love, and respect their husbands without fear of exploitation.

SEVEN

STEREOTYPES

A short time ago I was listening to a radio program. The guest that morning was a representative of a feminist organization lobbying against sex stereotyping of women in advertising. As she talked, she lashed out at males for degrading women by portraying them as housewives. She denounced advertising that is based on the assumption that it is the *woman* who cleans, cooks, and fulfills household responsibilities. Many people called in expressing similar sentiments. Near the end of the program, a quiet gentleman caller made a perceptive statement. Stereotyping, he said, is a problem common to all humanity and is not exclusive to women. Men are either portrayed as lazy, overweight, insensitive husbands who do nothing but watch T.V., or they are portrayed as promiscuous, playboy bachelors. Furthermore, he commented, blondes are stereotyped as being scatterbrained, policemen are stereotyped as being tough, teenagers are stereotyped as being rebellious . . . musicians, athletes, children, the aged, the rich, the poor — all are stereotyped. He concluded by saying that a group may escape one stereotype, but will eventually be branded with another which is just as likely to be unfair.

Stereotyping is mentally assigning a fixed form, behavior, and/or character to a person or group of persons. This process categorizes and thinks of people as conforming to one's fixed, conventional mental picture. Generally, there is some truth underlying stereotypes, but often we forget that people are unique individuals and that few conform perfectly to the images carried in our minds. In my life, I have worked as a janitor, secretary, fashion model, and medical professional. I have sung in rock bands, served as deaconess in my local church, coached sports, and taught seminars. Although I was the same person in each of these roles, people interacted with me differently depending on which role I was fulfilling at the time. For each role, people had preconceived ideas of my character and of how I should behave. Human nature produces stereotypes. Good or bad, right or wrong, the fact remains — stereotyping does occur.

Previously, women have been stereotyped as uneducated, pregnant housewives whose only goal in life was to have sparkling clean floors and bathtubs free from rings. To be sure, many working women resented being cast into the same category as their housewife peers. Today, the pendulum is swinging to the opposite and equally unfair extreme. Women who choose to stay at home are portrayed as deprived and unfulfilled. This fallacy is perpetuated by a new stereotype of women which the media is creating. Today, women are expected to be "superwomen," able to simultaneously manage a full-time career, a family, personal interests, and community involvement.

Stereotypes of women have changed as culture has changed. In Europe at the turn of the century, most women worked full-time in factories as well as bearing most of the household responsibilities. As unions came into existence, the conditions of work in the factories improved. The continent's economic climate also improved. The average standard of living rose and women were able to stay at home to raise children, while men provided for the family financially. This period, which was also reflected in North American postwar culture, gave birth to the barefoot, pregnant, tied-to-the-kitchen-sink stereotype of women. Today, some assume that the Bible expects women to conform to this very stereotype. They base this assumption on misconceptions regarding the role of submission, as well as misapplication of passages on childrearing and home management. Let us examine each of these misconceptions.

THE SUBMISSION STEREOTYPE

Submission is often mentally coupled with a quiet, introverted, and passive personality.[1] Since women are instructed in the Bible to be submissive to their husbands, we assume that God wants all women, regardless of personality type, to conform to this mental stereotype. Hence, women with energy, determination, resolve, ambition, and initiative are wrongly expected to change their personality. There is no Biblical evidence, however, that personality is, or should be, sex-related. Those who feel that God encourages all women to be sheepish, passive, introverted creatures and all men to be aggressive, domineering extroverts simply do not understand what the Bible is saying.

Scripture *does* direct believers to develop Christlike character traits such as patience, kindness, gentleness, meekness, and self-control, but these commands include *both* sexes. In fact, for every character directive given specifically to women, there is a corresponding one given to men (or to believers in general). For example, women are called upon to be quiet and gentle in their spirits (1 Peter 3:4); Colossians 3:12 mirrors this command for all believers (as well as Philippians 4:5; Galatians 5:23; 1 Timothy 6:11; 1 Peter 3:15; Matthew 5:5). Character traits are not Biblically assigned according to gender.

Submission for the woman does not imply changing personality. Here is a practical illustration of how different personalities would respond given the same situation.

Ann sees an advertisement for a continuing education course she is interested in attending. She discusses the idea with her husband and her husband replies: "I don't know, Honey, I wouldn't want you to take too much on . . . you work very hard, and you seem worn out by the end of the day. . . ."

Ann, a quiet, introverted woman replies, "I guess you're right — maybe next year."

Susan, on the other hand, is energetic, aggressive, and outgoing. She would counter such a reply with, "You're right about me being tired, but this is something I *want* to do. And unless you really object, I'm planning on taking the course. In fact, I've already filled out the application."

While these two women have entirely different personalities, they both are submissive to their husbands. Extroverted women do not have to change their personality in order to be submissive. These women, however, may have more difficulty than the quiet type in submitting to *final* decisions with which they disagree.

God does not have stereotypes. He views each woman as an individual and through His Spirit enables each individual with her unique personality to obey Him. Therefore, to mentally assign stereotypical behavior to the role of submission, and to expect *all* women to conform to a certain personality type, is not at all in line with New Testament teaching.

THE CHILDREARING STEREOTYPE

A second misconception is the idea that it is primarily the woman's role to bring up the children. Only three verses in the New Testament address the question of childrearing specifically in conjunction with women. Let us examine these verses.

1 Timothy 2:15

> But women will be [kept safe] saved through [the?] childbirth,
> if they continue in faith, love and holiness with propriety.

Despite a variety of interpretations, all commentators agree that this verse is extremely difficult to understand. Paul could have meant several things by it. The common proposals are as follows:

Women are saved from sin by bearing and raising children.

This interpretation suggests that women need to earn their salvation by bearing children. If true, this would contradict other clear New Testament passages which advocate salvation by grace alone (e.g., Ephesians 2:8, 9). This interpretation can be discarded if we adhere to the standard hermeneutical practice of small, obscure passages yielding to the larger, clear doctrinal passages.[2]

Childbirth refers to the birth of Christ.

The Greek word used for childbirth in 1 Timothy 2:15 is *teknogonia*. Apparently it is an unusual expression in which the use of the definite article is optional. Thus, it is a possibility that Paul was speaking about "the" childbirth — the specific childbirth of Christ the Messiah.[3] If this interpretation is correct, Paul would be saying:

Eve will be saved from the curse through the birth of the
promised child, Jesus, and other women who exhibit obedient
faith will be similarly saved.[4]

This interpretation is tenable.

Women will survive childbirth if they live holy lives.

This interpretation is unacceptable for two reasons. First, it is irrelevant to the context, as Paul here is discussing conduct and practice
in the local church. Furthermore, many holy women in the past have
died in childbirth, and many unholy women have had no difficulty
surviving it.

It is a continuation of the discussion of the role of women.

James Hurley suggests that the phrase in 1 Timothy 2:15 relates to
woman's role.[5] He points out that the context is a discussion of conduct for men and women in prayer, in adornment, and in teaching
and worship. Hurley suggests that Paul is thinking that Eve, and
women in general, will be saved or kept safe from wrongly seizing
men's role by embracing a woman's role (that of childbirth). Paul
thus speaks of childbirth as *representative* of the woman's role —
not as the role for every woman. When Paul speaks of childbirth, he
uses a typical part (i.e., childbearing) to represent the typical whole
(i.e., the role of women). Developments in our culture make his
selection of childbearing to represent the role of women seem inappropriate. However, in Paul's day, childbearing was viewed by both
men and women as an activity of surpassing personal and social
worth.[6] The bearing of children at that time was *central* to the
definition of womanhood. Paul may be paraphrased as saying:

> . . . that women in general (and most women in his day) will be
> kept safe from seizing men's role by participating in marital
> life (symbolized by childbirth), which should be accompanied
> by other hallmarks of Christian character (faith, love and holi-
> ness with propriety) which will produce the adornment of
> good deeds for which he called in 2:10.[7]

This view is also tenable.

Women are saved from loss of leadership.

A final possible interpretation of this passage is presented by Zane Hodges. He proposes that Paul is basing his comments here on Genesis 2 and 3. First, Paul argues that women are not to lead because it contradicts the order of creation (Genesis 2:18-25). Second, they have been denied leadership as a result of historical guilt — the woman is the first in the transgression (Genesis 3:1-6). Nevertheless, women will be saved from any loss of leadership through the child-bearing (i.e., all the godly seed in Christ — cf. Romans 16:20; Genesis 3:15). In sum, women are saved from any loss of leadership through the old adage that the hand that rocks the cradle rules the world. Hodges notes that Paul shifts from the singular to the plural: she, the woman, will be saved through the Childbearing (i.e., Christ and all His seed) if they (i.e., seed) continue in the faith.[8]

Although the last two interpretations are perhaps the best of the five, we cannot with absolute certainty state what Paul meant by 1 Timothy 2:15. Furthermore, the most probable interpretations do not support the thesis that women are primarily responsible for the child-rearing process. Therefore, this passage *cannot* be used as a proof-text for relegating the responsibility of childrearing solely to women.

1 Timothy 5:10, 14

The only other verses in the New Testament which speak specifically of women with regard to childbearing and/or childrearing are 1 Timothy 5:10 and 14. Verse 9 is included for clarity.

> No widow may be put on the list of widows unless she is over sixty, has been faithful to her husband, and is well known for her good deeds, such as bringing up children, showing hospitality, washing the feet of the saints, helping those in trouble and devoting herself to all kinds of good deeds. . . . So I counsel younger widows to marry, to have children, to manage their homes and to give the enemy no opportunity for slander.

The list of widows was apparently an organized effort to care for those widows who had no means of financial support. This was a type of welfare roll that ensured that their needs were provided for. Older widows were put on this list if they were over sixty years of age, if they had been faithful to their husbands, and if they had done "good deeds" during their lifetime. Childrearing, as well as washing the feet of the saints, are listed as examples of such good deeds. It is important to note that these are merely *examples* of good deeds and not imperatives.

Likewise, verse 14 addresses the question of enrollment of younger widows on this list. Paul's counsel to younger widows was to remarry and have children. His reason for this was that it would help them avoid the common pitfalls to which young widows are susceptible. These pitfalls include idleness, gossiping, and meddling in other people's affairs. Paul was also concerned that the younger widows would have difficulty remaining single; therefore, he advised not to put them on the list. Again, childbearing/childrearing is not demanded of these women, although both are suggested and seen as a natural consequence of marriage.

Therefore, in context 1 Timothy 2:15 and 5:10, 14 do not support the idea that it is only the woman's job to raise children.

More often than not, childrearing is addressed in the Bible as a *mutual* responsibility of *both* parents.[9] Furthermore, argument can be presented that it is the *men* who are expected to play the *major* role in children's discipline and instruction (Ephesians 6:4; Proverbs 3:12; 15:5; Colossians 3:21; 1 Timothy 3:4, 12; Hebrews 12:9). Thus, Scripture negates the stereotype that childrearing is primarily the wife's responsibility.

THE HOME MANAGEMENT STEREOTYPE

The final stereotype which we will address is that of the "woman's place being in the home." The passage presented to support this concept is Titus 2:4, 5:

> Then they [older women] can train the younger women to love their husbands and children, to be self-controlled and pure, to be busy at home, to be kind, and to be subject to their husbands so that no one will malign the word of God.

Many people have used the phrase "to be busy at home" to contend that women with children should not have employment out-

side the home. Although I am supportive of mothers who choose to
stay at home full-time with their children and believe that doing so
is wise, I am not convinced that Titus 2:4, 5 can be used as a proof-
text to prescribe that all women stay at home full-time.

The Greek word for the phrase "to be busy at home" literally
means home-workers.[10] Arndt and Ginrich state that its verb form
indicates fulfilling one's household duties.[11] In addition to this
verse, 1 Timothy 5:14 and Proverbs 31 indicate support for the concept of the woman carrying responsibility for home management.
Although this duty is shared by the male (1 Timothy 3:4-5, 12), the
primary responsibility does seem to fall on the woman.

The above verses indicate that women *do* have responsibility in
the home. However, the specifics of their duties and how they are to
be discharged are not given in Scripture. Thus, women are not limited to working in the home, but are encouraged to ensure that household duties are fulfilled and that the household is properly managed.

Although the woman has the primary responsibility to manage
the home, she does not have to *do* everything in the home. The Bible
does not present the concept of a sex-based division of labor.
Husbands are just as capable at fulfilling practical household tasks
such as doing dishes, running errands, and going shopping. Cooking
is definitely *not* a God-ordained female task. Wives need to sit down
with their husbands and work out an agreeable division of labor for
their own homes. This division will differ from home to home, from
individual to individual, and will likely change depending on what
phase of life the family unit is at. For example, when my husband and
I were both working full-time, he did the vacuuming and dusting, and
I did the laundry. We shared responsibility for cooking. Prior to the
birth of our first child, I quit work and stayed at home. At that time, I
assumed many of his household duties. After I had the baby, he reas-
sumed some duties. At this point in our lives, it is economically more
feasible for me to stay home with the children and for him to work
outside the home. Yet, there may come a time in the future when our
duties will be reversed. Who does what is not the point. The point is
that everything is done. Women are not to neglect their responsibility
of ensuring that the home is managed. Whether they, their husbands,
or someone else actually does the work is inconsequential.

The Bible is not concerned with specifics of who does what.

However, God *is* concerned with all wrong action which would discredit Christianity. Titus 2:5 says that women should be trained to be busy at home "so that *no one will malign the word of God.*" Similarly, 1 Timothy 5:14 counsels younger widows to have children and to manage their homes *"to give the enemy no opportunity for slander."* Women who neglect their homes and families are being irresponsible witnesses to the rest of the world. God disapproves of neglect.

Women with children must be particularly careful not to be neglectful. God has given us children as a trust, and Christian parents must ensure that godly morals and character are instilled into their lives. For this reason, strong argument can be made for the necessity of a parent's constant presence during a child's early, formative years and continuing availability throughout the child's school years. Although the Bible does not *dictate* that women with children stay at home, it does hold parents responsible for the proper upbringing of their children. This definitely involves placing the family's welfare as priority over one's personal career. For the Christian woman, staying at home with children may be indicated, as this action may be in the best interest of the family unit.

Paul encourages women to be busy at home in order to avoid the sins of idleness, gossip, and meddling. I feel the emphasis is not for women to be (busy at) HOME, but for women to BE BUSY (at home). For the Christian woman, this means fulfilling her responsibilities at home although she may also work outside of the home. God has set marriage and the family unit as the foundational building blocks for the Christian community. The family unit is to be a strong example to the rest of the world. Women who neglect their homes, their family, or their marriage discredit Christ.

To summarize, the Bible does not support stereotypes, and it does not deny women careers. The woman in Proverbs 31 was involved in travel, charity, business, and commerce. Lydia was a seller of dyes, Priscilla was a tentmaker, and Dorcas was a dressmaker. Women can work inside or outside the home. They can mop floors or shingle roofs, they can be introverts or extroverts, they can be single or married. All are within the boundaries of God's Word. God is not concerned with the specifics of who does what. However, God is concerned that women fulfill their responsibility in the home, and that their actions in no way discredit Christianity or His created order.

BACK TO THE GARDEN

New Testament marital roles can be summarized as directing women and men "back to the garden." The unity and harmony which characterized the first male-female relationship is a model for all believers. Christ's death on the cross has enabled Christians to overcome the sin nature that causes misuse of and rebellion against the created order. In the New Testament, wives are called upon to willingly submit to their husbands, and husbands are called upon to provide loving, servant-leadership for their wives.

The marital role directives in the New Testament are not given as punishment nor as a burden. God gave these to Christian couples to liberate them. Marriages that function according to God's plan have a unity that far surpasses the give-and-take "equal" marriage plans prescribed by our society. God's plan works, and it works for our own good! We do not need to fear obeying His instructions for male-female roles. Marriage is *fun*, fulfilling, and satisfying when lived by God's design. That is how it is meant to be!

God's plan for marital roles is the same as it was at the creation of man and woman. God desires that husbands and wives enjoy each other and that they live in harmony and unity. The way this is achieved is a paradox. Men are not to demand submission. They are to sacrificially serve and love their wives. Wives are not to demand equal rights. They are to willingly submit to their husbands. The unity and harmony which can result is profound. New Testament marital roles definitely point us back to Eden, back to the "place of pleasure."

PART THREE:

GOD'S ORDER IN THE CHURCH

EIGHT

THE ROLE OF WOMEN IN THE CHURCH

Jesus was a feminist to a degree far beyond that of His fellows and followers. . . . No other Western prophet, seer, or would-be redeemer of humanity was so devoted to the feminine half of mankind.[1]

Charles Seltman

While we may or may not agree with Seltman's categorization of Jesus as a feminist, it is obvious that Jesus Christ's attitude toward women was revolutionary. He treated them as equals and coheirs in the gospel. He passed this attitude on to His apostles, for in New Testament churches, women played a *vital* role, and their worth and contribution were not questioned. Women formed the nucleus of the assembly in Philippi (Acts 16:11-15) and played central roles in the establishment of assemblies in Thessalonica (Acts 17:4) and Berea (Acts 17:12). Many women are cited as hostesses of homes in which the believers gathered (Acts 12:12; 16:15; 1 Corinthians 16:19; Colossians 4:15; Philemon 2). Furthermore, the women in the early church also exercised a variety of spiritual gifts. Euodia, Syntyche (Philippians 4:2, 3), Lydia (Acts 16:15), and Priscilla (Acts 18:2, 26; Romans 16:3) were gifted in evangelism. Priscilla is shown to have done some private teaching of Apollos (Acts 18:26). Lois and Eunice instructed Timothy (2 Timothy 1:5; 3:14, 15). Older women were *expected* to teach younger ones (Titus 2:3-5). The four daughters of Philip the evangelist (Acts 21:9) had the gift of prophecy. Gifts of good deeds and hospitality were also

shown by numerous women (Acts 9:36; 1 Timothy 5:10). In addition, women were actively involved in prayer. They prayed together
with men in small groups (Acts 1:14; 12:12). They also exercised
personal prayer ministry (1 Timothy 5:5). Women played an important part in spiritual ministry within the family context and were also
involved in pastoral-type ministry to others. This ministry included
the care of believers, their nurture and growth in the Lord, as well as
counseling and visiting.

Women in the New Testament churches were not mere specta-
tors. They played an active, vibrant, and vital role in the day-to-day
functioning of the body of believers. Unfortunately, it seems as
though women's role in the church has diminished in past centuries.
While there are many facets to male and female roles within the
body of believers, women often end up in service roles (pouring
punch, wrapping bandages for missionaries, and teaching Sunday
school) and are excluded from the areas of teaching adults, administration, and leadership. The church has been guilty of attempting
to squeeze all women into an identical ministry mold, frustrating
those who are not so inclined or gifted. Consequently, discussion
regarding the role of women has centered on the appointment, or
ordination, of women to official leadership offices.

Denominational statistics reflect that in the past two decades,
there has been a major doctrinal shift towards the ordination of
women. Almost every group now allows women as well as men to
occupy official leadership positions. In 1980, for example, the general assembly of the United Presbyterian Church, USA, deemed the
appointment of women elders compulsory. Each congregation is
now *required* to "ordain" both male and female elders. The general
council of the Assemblies of God in 1977 listed 1600 ordained
women. In 1978, The Lutheran Church in America ordained more
than ninety women as Lutheran ministers. Presently, United
Methodist churches allow and promote women elders and women
bishops. The American Baptist Convention and Southern Baptist
Convention allow female pastors. In fact, the only major Protestant
denomination in the United States which does not allow for the ordination of women is the Lutheran Church Missouri Synod. But it too
has been advised by a task force on women to reconsider its
position.[2]

Even the Catholic Church has not been immune to this movement. Pope John Paul II has received much criticism regarding his
firm stance on the role of women. In Canada, a national organization
called Canadian Catholics for Women's Ordination exists exclusively to oppose his views. It is the counterpart to many other
national organizations (such as The National Coalition of Nuns —
USA) that condemn the revised code of canon law prohibiting ordination of women.[3] Without question, during the last twenty years,
the issue of women leading the church has become prominent,
volatile, and persuasive.

Although I realize that the church has often frustrated women
by limiting their service, I cannot agree with the current solution to
this problem. While God does *not* want women to bury their talents
or waste their gifts, it is wrong to misappropriate Scripture to
accommodate the way *we* think those gifts should be exercised. The
inclusion of women in official leadership roles within the church is
simply not supported by Scripture.

The principle of headship, which structures the marital relationship, is also evidenced within the church. It is this principle
which is honored by the roles assigned to male and female in the
body of believers. As in marriage, male and female are equal in
terms of their worth as individuals, but they are assigned specific
roles and functions.

Advocates of female ordination object to this sex-specific
classification. They cite the numerous examples of women's
involvement in the New Testament church. Then because the
Gospels and Acts do not explicitly command *men* to lead in the
local church, they assume that *women* have the inalienable right to
do so. Also, they gloss over or dismiss passages in the epistles that
directly prohibit women from this function.

This method of dealing with Scripture is awkward. For the key
to interpreting references to women in the Gospels and Acts and the
personal references to them in the epistles is the specific teaching in
the epistles.[4] In other words, one must *first* look at the specific
teaching on the subject, and *then* look at the example of the early
church. Basing one's theology on examples, as they are perceived,
and then bending clear teaching to conform to one's perceptions is
a case of putting the cart before the horse. The task before us is to

harmonize the clear doctrinal teaching in the epistles with the rich vastness of women's involvement cited in the Gospels and Acts.

While the epistles undeniably maintain the equality of men and women, they limit the role of women in the guidance of, and public assembly of, the body of believers. Women are not allowed to be elders, nor are they encouraged to participate vocally in the public meeting which includes the Lord's Supper. Finally, in recognition of the principle of headship and male leadership, they are to "veil" themselves in the assembly meeting. The passages which teach this are 1 Corinthians 11:3ff., 14:33, 1 Timothy 2:11, 12 as well as 1 Timothy 3, Titus 1, and 1 Peter 5 (which limit the role of overseers and deacons to *men*).

While women in the early church were vitally involved in ministry, their activity in the public gathering of Christians (or in today's terms — the Sunday morning meeting) *was* carefully regulated in the epistles. The very fact that such regulations were needed shows how much women shared in the life of the New Testament church. These regulations did not supersede, but supplemented the principle of equal privilege for women so clearly announced by Christianity.[5] However this equality did not mean men and women had the same function and responsibility. It was in the public meeting of the church where this was evidenced most clearly. The "sign" women were to wear on their heads during worship, their limited verbal participation, and their absence from official leadership roles visibly showed adherence to God's created order.

The teaching regarding the role of women in the church is difficult to understand in contemporary society. The reason, I believe, is that the church today has strayed from its Biblical blueprint. Modern churches, to varying degrees, often neglect the New Testament pattern of church leadership, the priesthood of believers, and spiritual gifts. The sad reality is that many churches are only a dull reflection of the New Testament church. And women, unfortunately, seem to have suffered the most by this departure.

The next few chapters deal with sensitive issues. I have tried to be honest and accurate. Because I am a woman, I am aware that some of the teaching may touch raw nerves. Nevertheless, I feel that one of the greatest needs of the church today is for women to understand their God-given role. In order to deal with New Testament teaching on the role of women in the church, I have divided this section topically. I will begin by discussing Paul's teaching on the custom of "veiling." The rationale he presents for this custom points to the principle of headship within the church. This principle underlies male/female role directives and will serve as a base for the following topics of women's verbal participation in the church and the participation of women in the formal offices of the church. After discussing the Biblical instruction on the role of women in the church, I will critique feminist theology. Finally, I will present my own view on how to rectify the problem of the degradation of the role of women within the church.

HEADSHIP AND
HEAD COVERINGS

The principle of headship is the ground in which New Testament directives for female and male roles within the church are rooted. The most extensive Bible passage dealing with this principle is found in Paul's first letter to the Corinthians, chapter eleven. Here we will begin our discussion about the role of women in the church:

> I praise you for remembering me in everything and for holding to the teachings, just as I passed them on to you. Now I want you to realize that the head of every man is Christ, and the head of the woman is man, and the head of Christ is God. Every man who prays or prophesies with his head covered dishonors his head. And every woman who prays or prophesies with her head uncovered dishonors her head — it is just as though her head were shaved. If a woman does not cover her head, she should have her hair cut off; and if it is a disgrace for a woman to have her hair cut or shaved off, she should cover her head. A man ought not to cover his head, since he is the image and glory of God; but the woman is the glory of man. For man did not come from woman, but woman from man; neither was man created for woman, but woman for man. For this reason, and because of the angels, the woman ought to have a sign of authority on her head.

In the Lord, however, woman is not independent of man,
nor is man independent of woman. For as woman came from
man, so also man is born of woman. But everything comes
from God. Judge for yourselves: Is it proper for a woman to
pray to God with her head uncovered? Does not the very
nature of things teach you that if a man has long hair, it is a
disgrace to him, but that if a woman has long hair, it is her
glory? For long hair is given to her as a covering. If anyone
wants to be contentious about this, we have no other practice
— nor do the churches of God. (1 Corinthians 11:2-16)

In this passage, Paul instructed the Corinthians in a practice
which was to reflect the principle of headship. The practice was the
"veiling" of the Corinthian women in the public assembly of believers. Although this practice appears trivial on the surface, much can
be gleaned by closer scrutiny. In fact, Paul's rationale for the custom
of veiling, or head coverings, buttresses the New Testament teaching on the role of women in the church. Understanding this practice
and Paul's defense of it will thus lay a foundation for the remainder
of our study.

THE SITUATION AT CORINTH

In Corinth were Christians of many backgrounds — Jewish, Greek,
Roman, and Germanic. In this cultural mosaic were many customs
regarding the wearing of coverings in the church worship meeting.
Greek men prayed with their heads uncovered and Jewish and
Roman men with their heads covered.[1] As far as females were concerned, scholars are uncertain whether the cultural mores in Corinth
dictated universal veiling. The general consensus at present is that
head coverings in public were mandatory for Jewish women, but not
for Greek and Roman women.[2]

In 1 Corinthians, Paul is commending the Christians for adhering to the practice that he had taught them: the women were to be
covered in the public meeting of the church and the men were not.
This practice symbolized the principle of headship woven into the
created order. The instructions Paul gave the Corinthian church did
not correspond to any Greco-Roman custom at that time, although

it probably reflected the practice followed by Jewish women in public.

In Corinth, the believers were apparently wondering about the reasons for keeping the custom of head coverings. Why they wondered is not clear, but it is likely that there was a growing insurgence against the custom. The insurgence may have been inspired, in part, by a false understanding of Christian freedom.

The Corinthian Christians made much of their newfound freedom in Christ (1 Corinthians 4:8-10). The problem at Corinth could have been an overemphasis on the freedom which had ensued from the spiritual equality of Christian women.[3] It is possible that the Corinthian women felt that their new position in Christ, and their resultant freedom, were incompatible with wearing a sign of submission.[4]

Another possible factor was spiritual giftedness. In 1 Corinthians 1:7, we are told that the church at Corinth lacked no spiritual gift. Thus, it is likely that some women in that church had the gift of teaching and had assumed that they should be exercising it in the public worship meeting. Because the veil, which represented submission, was incompatible with public teaching, some women were discarding the practice.

Paul argues that freedom in Christ does not allow the rejection of God's order and the particular expression of it.[5] Paul corrects any misconception of freedom by teaching that in the church, as in marriage, there is freedom for all, yet concurrent, distinctive roles for the sexes. He thus admonishes the Corinthians to uphold the practice of head coverings and elaborates on the principle which head coverings reflect.

THE PRINCIPLE AT STAKE

From our vantage point, Paul appears rather fanatical about head coverings. This fanaticism, however, was not centered on the practice itself, but rather on the underlying principle it exemplified. Paul taught the Corinthian believers that the covering of women in the worship meeting symbolized the principle of *headship*. According to Paul, the discarding of this symbol went far beyond mere cosmetic adjustment. It was an affront to the order God had instituted at creation.

In 1 Corinthians 11:3, Paul teaches that a hierarchy of head-ship authority is ordered: God-Christ-man-woman. The most legit-imate meaning for the word *headship* is authority over. In 1 Corinthians 11:3, the man/woman relationship is sandwiched between two other relationships that are unquestionably hierarchi-cal: Christ as head of man, and God as head of Christ. In context then, Paul is speaking of hierarchical relationships. He apparently viewed the head covering as symbolic of woman's relation to man's authority within hierarchical order.[6] Paul taught that headship/authority is fundamental to the marital relationship and to the ques-tion of head coverings. According to Paul, the discarding of head coverings for women in worship represented the rejection of God's created order. Thus, headship was the Biblical issue at stake.

THE PRACTICE TAUGHT

There has been some discussion as to the type of covering Paul had in mind for women. One view is that 1 Corinthians 11 refers to hair length and/or hair style. Verse 15 is often cited. In this verse, Paul states that "long hair is given to her [woman] as a covering." Thus, casual readers assert that if a woman has long hair, she needn't cover her head in the assembly meeting.

A more accurate position is that Paul intended a veil or shawl or garment to be worn upon the head. Verse 14 refers to the reason of nature in support of wearing a head covering. Thus, verse 15 is an extension of Paul's argument. Long hair is natural for a woman, and according to Paul, this example in nature adds evidence that women should wear an artificial covering in the assembly meeting. In verse 6, he reasons that if a woman wants to neglect the artificial covering, she might as well go all the way and get rid of her natural covering by shaving her head: "If a woman does not cover her head, she should have her hair cut off; and if it is a disgrace for a woman to have her hair cut or shaved off, she should cover her head."

Verse 6 does not make sense if we maintain that hair is the only covering required. Paul would be saying: "If a woman doesn't cover her head with hair, she should have her hair cut off; and if it is a disgrace for a woman to have her hair cut or shaved off, she should cover her head with hair."

Interpreting covering as long hair reduces verse 6 to absurdity. Paul's meaning in verse 15 is not that a woman's long hair is adequate covering, but that her natural covering indicates that an artificial covering is an appropriate expression of God's order. "If a woman will be so shameless as to appear without said covering, let her act consistently, and give such a token of her shamelessness as will be seen in stripping her head entirely of hair."[7] Paul is basically saying that the logical extension of not wearing a head covering during worship is appearing bald. Furthermore, interpreting hair as the only covering necessary does not meet the demands of the Biblical text. To indicate a covering, Paul used the word *katakalupto*, which literally means to cover oneself.[8] The noun form of the same word is found in 2 Corinthians 3:13-16, and it literally means something upon the head. Historically, this was understood to be a robe, linen cloth, or some other kind of physical covering. Paul uses a different word in verse 15 for hair as a natural covering than he does in verses 4-7 for the artificial covering.[9]

One recent commentator, James Hurley, thinks that the covering refers to a woman's hair style. He states that women should have long hair and wear it in a bun or pinned up when praying or prophesying. Hurley builds a logical argument, but his conclusions are tenuous because the premises for his argument are based on an obscure Old Testament reading of the word.[10] It should be noted that if one follows his conclusions, then all women should have long hair and should wear it pinned up in church.

In summary, the most natural and consistent view is that Paul taught that women should wear something upon their heads. Whether this was a shawl, a veil, or some sort of a garment is unclear.

When were the head coverings to be worn? All of chapters 11 to 14 deal with the local church meeting. Phrases such as "when you come together" and "the body" and "your meeting" indicate this clearly (see 11:18, 20, 33; 12:12, 28; 14:19, 24, 26, 33, 34). In these passages, Paul addressed the question of head coverings along with the Lord's Supper, unity of believers in the body, spiritual gifts, prophecy, tongues, and orderly worship. Therefore, his teaching on head coverings applied specifically to the public gathering of the entire community of believers for worship. Apparently, small group meetings or informal get-togethers were excluded.

Furthermore, Paul directed women to be covered in the assembly meeting when praying or prophesying. Paul was here addressing the question of head coverings and not the question of woman's participation in the meeting. This was not a license for free participation on the part of women. Paul recognized that there would be occasions when a woman would participate in the assembly meeting in prayer or sharing. On such occasions the woman was to have a sign of authority on her head.

THE REASONS GIVEN

In this passage are six reasons for women wearing head coverings and men not wearing them. Each reason endorses the principle of headship.

The Reason of Divine Order (vs. 3)

According to verse 3, the order of headship is sequenced: God-Christ-man-woman. This is an obvious hierarchy. Yet it is a hierarchy of authority/submission relationships that exists alongside the concept of equality. Notice in verses 11, 12 that Paul is careful to draw male attention to the proper perspective: "In the Lord, however, woman is not independent of man, nor is man independent of woman. For as woman came from man, so also man is born of woman. But everything comes from God."

Paul is reminding the men that the headship concept and the hierarchical structure do not reflect superiority and inferiority. Woman and man are dependent on each other, and all are dependent on God. They are equal in spiritual privileges. However, men and women are to respect and adhere to the created hierarchical order. The head covering is a symbol of this order. Thus, the woman who wore a head covering visually showed that she recognized herself to be under authority. For the man to wear a symbol of authority on his head in worship would imply that he had abdicated the sovereignty and dignity given him by the Creator. For the woman to neglect to do so would be to deny her relationship to man and God as ordained in creation.[11]

The Reason of the Order of Creation (vv. 8, 9)

Adam was created first. Eve was created from and for Adam. Chronologically then, male was created before female. The male was thus the eldest or the firstborn of human beings.

The firstborn child in the family unit has traditionally possessed certain rights. Genesis 27 describes Jacob tricking his older brother Esau out of his birthright and blessing — two rights ascribed to the firstborn of the family. Esau had claim to these rights, not because he was worthier than Jacob, but simply because of his position as firstborn. "The law of the firstborn" is discussed in Deuteronomy 21:15-17. Apparently, the position of firstborn carries with it authority. In Colossians 1:15-18 we are told that Christ has authority because He was the firstborn over all creation. Paul asserts that Adam's status as the oldest carried with it the leadership appropriate to a first-born son.[12] God has also ascribed this place of authority to men after Adam. Their position has nothing to do with their intellect, ability, or spirituality, but is based on the order of creation. In 1 Timothy 2:13, 14 Paul uses the same argument: Man was created first, and the resultant role for women is one of submission. This submission was to be symbolized by the head covering.

The Reason of Divine Glory (vs. 7)

Verse 7 states that "man ought not to cover his head, since he is the image and glory of God; but the woman is the glory of man." Man and woman are both created in the image of God. This is clear in Genesis, and Paul seems to take it for granted in verse 7. The difference between man and woman is that man is the "glory of God," and woman is the "glory of man." Bullinger says that the Greek word used here denotes "the appearance of glory attracting the gaze, manifestation of glory."[13] Hurley explains that "the concept of glory deals with the showing or manifesting of the role or station of another."[14] Thus, man honors the rule of God by being subordinate to Him and by headship over his wife. The wife is the glory of her husband as she honors *his* headship by her life and attitude.[15] Paul's argument then is that the glory of God should not be veiled in the presence of God, but that the glory of man should be veiled in the presence of God during corporate worship. The created order should first be realized and then visibly demonstrated.[16]

Because of the Angels (vs. 10)

Paul also instructs believers to follow the head covering practice on account, or in consideration of, the angels. Superficially, this argument appears irrelevant, but a closer examination shows otherwise.

Angels are God's messengers. Their supreme characteristic is total and immediate obedience to God.[17] Throughout Scripture, they are shown as creatures who possess power, but are submissive to God's will. Angels themselves are ranked in hierarchical orders, or legions. Good angels, who saw the serious breach of divine order when Satan revolted, are carefully observing the Church to see whether it is properly maintaining God's order.[18] Paul argues that it is proper for a woman to cover her head as a sign of subordination because of the angels, in order that these most submissive of all creatures will not be offended by lack of submission.[19]

Furthermore, the Bible tells that that the angels were present at creation (Job 38:7) to be witnesses of God's unique design for man and woman and therefore would be offended at any violation of that order.[20] The Midrash, a collection of rabbinic writings commenting on the Old Testament, teaches that the angels are the guardians of the created order. Perhaps God's people are being watched by the angels to see if they are properly fulfilling this order (Ephesians 3:9, 10). Paul wanted women to give due regard to the created order because of the angels. One way women showed regard for this order was by wearing head coverings during worship.

The Reason from Nature (vv. 13-15)

Paul appeals to nature for the fifth reason for head coverings. He is saying that "by nature" man should be exposed before God, and "by nature" woman should be covered before God. It is natural for a woman's hair to be longer than a man's. A man need not be embarrassed at having little hair, or even no hair at all, but to a woman it is a shame.

It is generally true throughout the world that a man's hair (even if the styles are long) can be too long. It can be a shame to him. Long hair can never be a shame to a woman. This is not merely cultural, for women by nature have longer hair than men. Therefore, Paul is saying that women have been given a sign of subordination by nature itself. The veil, or covering, is to be the conventional expression of this principle. It is to be worn in the assembly meeting to recognize that God intended by nature for women to show their subordination by being covered. Nature provides an analogy for head coverings, an analogy that should have helped believers see that head coverings for women were an appropriate way to express their God-given role during worship.[21]

The Reason of Universality of Christian Practice (vs. 16)

The final reason Paul cites for the practice of head coverings is that of universal Christian practice. Apparently, the veiling or covering of women in worship was a universal practice of the churches established by the apostles. Therefore, we see Paul saying, "If anyone wants to be contentious about this, we have no other practice — nor do the churches of God"(vs.16).

This verse does not say, "If you want to argue about this, don't bother, because it isn't that important, and neither I nor the churches follow it anyway." The sense is: "I have never permitted the custom of unveiled praying or prophesying by women, and no church has introduced it."[22] Paul taught all the churches this custom and he expected them to follow it. In this final statement he cuts off all further argument by appealing to universal Christian usage.[23]

To summarize, the reasons Paul gives to support the custom of head coverings and its underlying principle of headship are powerful. They are based on the act of creation and natural law. They illustrate the centrality of headship to male and female roles in the church.

APPLICATION TO SINGLE WOMEN

A head covering symbolically acknowledged woman's position in the created order. It expressed the headship inherent in the marital relationship and in the church. Because the head covering reflected hierarchy in marriage, there may have been some question as to its validity for single women.

There are many reasons to believe that Paul thought the head covering symbol appropriate for single women. To begin, the Greek words Paul uses for man and woman have more general connotations of male and female rather than husbands and wives. Moreover, the hair length illustration used indicates that he thought the ruling applied to all. Otherwise, the illustration loses its force, since hair length applied to all women, not just married ones.[24] Hence, while the central focus of the passage is husbands and wives, other women and other men followed the same patterns because their identities as women and men were more fundamental than their unmarried state.[25] The universal applicability of headship and the head covering symbol did not, however, imply that every woman was to submit to every and any man! Women were commanded to submit to their husbands and to their husbands only. They would of course submit in other hierarchical relationships, such as to the elders of church, just as men would. But to say that the Bible directs all women to obey all men is going beyond what this passage teaches and beyond the symbolism of the head covering.

Therefore, single women were also to recognize the hierarchy of male-female relationships God had ordered in creation. By wearing a covering, a single woman stated: "I recognize that God has ordered women to submit within the marriage relationship. Even though I am not married, I understand this principle, and I show my respect for it by wearing a head covering. Even if I never marry, I wear a symbol which recognizes my place in creation."

The head covering of women in worship was a symbol of God's order in creation. It was an obvious symbol which showed respect for the principle of headship. Paul taught a Christological hierarchy which was to be reflected in the public assembly in a visible way — by the veiling of women and bare heads of men. He wanted both men and women to fulfill their appointed roles. To Paul, rejection of the head covering did not reflect equality, but rather rejection of divine ordinance.

HEADSHIP AND HEAD COVERINGS — FOR TODAY?

Many modern writers question the applicability of headship and the headship symbolism to our age.[26] They often quote 1 Corinthians 11:2: ("I praise you for remembering me in everything and for holding to the traditions [or teachings], just as I passed them on to you") in defense of their argument. Paul's teachings are to be viewed as traditions which will evolve and change in response to the cultural situation.

It is often assumed that traditions are something unexamined, followed simply out of habit, that is, for no good reason. However, Paul did not view his teaching that way. "In the Pauline writings, words like *tradition* (*paradosis*), *delivered* (*paradidomai*), and *maintain* (*katechein*), and possibly in this context *remember* (*mimneskomai*), refer to a very serious approach to tradition. Along with *receive* (*paralambanein*) and (*kratein*), these words indicate a careful process of preserving truths from one generation to another."[27] Thus, when Paul speaks about traditions, he does not mean some kind of social conformity but a serious process of passing on a way of life. For this reason, the Bible translators who use the word *teachings* instead of *traditions* more accurately reflect the actual meaning of the word. Headship cannot be dismissed as inapplicable on the basis of Paul's reference to its symbolism as a tradition.

Are Paul's instructions applicable? To some they appear applicable in principle — to others not. And what about head coverings and submission? How can we know if these are meant for us? Since we are products of our culture, it is easy to slip into dismissing Biblical principles and practices as inapplicable because they are not understood or are not popular in contemporary society. Yet we must avoid dismissing any such practices without careful study first to ascertain if they do indeed apply to all cultures.

Some logical steps that assist us in translating Biblical commands from one culture and time to another have been summarized by Henry A. Virkler in *Hermeneutics: Principles and Processes of Biblical Interpretation:*[28]

1. Discern as accurately as possible the principle behind the command.

2. Discern whether the principle is cross-cultural or culture-bound by examining the reasons given for the principle.

3. If a principle is cross-cultural, determine whether or not the same behavioral application in our culture will express the principle as adequately and accurately as the Biblical one.

4. If the behavioral expression of a principle should be changed, suggest a cultural equivalent that will express the God-given principle behind the original command.

5. If, after careful study, the nature of the Biblical principle and its attendant command remain in question, apply the Biblical precept of humility. It is better to treat a principle and command as

cross-cultural and be guilty of being overscrupulous in our desire to obey God than to treat it as culture-bound and come short of what God requires.

Let us work through the above guidelines with regard to the custom endorsed by Paul in 1 Corinthians 11. First, we identify the principles behind the command of the veiling of women as hierarchical order and male headship. The reasons given for headship are derived from the created order. These transcend time.[29] Headship is as applicable to us as it was in Paul's day.

As a third step, we must determine whether head coverings are an appropriate expression of the principle of headship today. On this point, two opinions prevail. Some evangelical scholars feel that head coverings were relevant only in Paul's culture. They point out that Jewish women in Corinth covered their heads in public. Jews usually made up part of the membership of the churches Paul founded (a ruler of the synagogue was one of Paul's first converts in Corinth — Acts 18). To these believers, the veil was extremely significant and was logically the most appropriate symbol of male headship. It communicated a demeanor humble and submissive to male leadership. Women's adornment, or clothing, differentiated them from men. Their failure to wear the head covering during worship signalled rebellion.

However, head coverings seem to have no meaning in today's culture, and failure to wear them sends no message to the congregation. But the difference between male and female roles in the church *does* need to be evidenced. Scholars who hold to this first view suggest that an appropriate expression of headship today is dress that clearly defines masculinity and femininity. The *principle* of headship is affirmed without qualification, but the *way* the principle is expressed is open to a variety of expressions to reflect the diversity of the human situation.[30]

The second view on the relevance of head coverings is that these are, in fact, the most appropriate expression of headship today. Paul never refers to the practices or customs of his day in his argument for head coverings. This is notable, for it is often said that head coverings for Christian women were necessary in Paul's culture so as not to offend the status quo.[31] But since the practice of head coverings as described in 1 Corinthians 11 was not a particular Greek,

Asian, or Roman custom, and since the Corinthian congregation was Greco-Roman, this argument is seen as invalid. Failure to wear head coverings would have caused no scandal to the local population. Furthermore, in 1 Corinthians 11 Paul gives reasons which not only explain the principle of headship but its behavioral expression — head coverings. For example, his appeal to nature and the natural covering of women indicate that he believed the veiling of women to be the most appropriate expression of male headship. Therefore, the second view concludes that no behavioral expression reflects the principle of headship more adequately than the expression Paul himself designates. Both the principle and its commanded behavioral expression are seen as applicable today.[32]

SUMMARY

In 1 Corinthians 11, Paul exhorts the Corinthian church to adhere to a custom he had taught them: Women were to veil themselves in the public assembly of believers, and men were not. This was a distinctly Christian custom observed out of respect for the principle of headship. The reasons Paul gives for this custom are cross-cultural. They appeal to creation and the laws of nature. This reveals to us how intricately the principle of headship is woven into the created order. Whether one believes that women should veil themselves today (as I would encourage) or that headship could be affirmed by other appropriate forms of dress in our day, the conclusion is the same: The headship principle is so fundamental, so central to the functioning of the local church that it must be be evidenced symbolically in the Christian meeting. Headship is the same principle which underlies marital structure. And this vital doctrine lays foundation for the balance of New Testament teaching on the role of women in the church.

VERBAL PARTICIPATION

Today women are publicly speaking out against everything from pornography to nuclear war. To us it seems odd that Scripture should address the question of women's verbal participation in church. Why did the Apostle Paul address this topic? Did the women in his time abuse their freedom? Or was it culturally inappropriate for them to speak? And is there a possibility that Paul's instructions have application to our day and age?

Although an unbiased evaluation of the topic is difficult, the teachings on woman's verbal participation in the church meeting are vital to the understanding of woman's role in the church. These passages augment and verify Paul's discourse on woman's role as it pertains to headship and church leadership.

> As in all the congregations of the saints, women should remain silent in the churches. They are not allowed to speak, but must be in submission, as the Law says. If they want to inquire about something, they should ask their own husbands at home; for it is disgraceful for a woman to speak in the church. Did the word of God originate with you? Or are you the only people it has reached? (1 Corinthians 14:33b-36)

CONTEXT

First Corinthians chapters 11-14 give the pattern for the local church meeting. The fourteenth chapter presents guidelines for various kinds of public speech during that meeting. In this chapter, the Greek word for speech (*lalein*) and its various forms appear twenty-four times. For example, in verse 28, a man who speaks (*lalei*) in a tongue must be silent (*sigato*) unless there is an interpreter. In verses 29, 30, prophets are to speak (*laletosan*), but are to be silent (*sigato*) if someone receives a revelation. Similarly in verse 34, women are *not* to speak (*laleo*), but are to remain silent (*sigato*). The verse in which Paul limits women's speech resides in a passage that addresses all types of speech in the local church meeting.

QUELLING THE INJUNCTION

My immediate reaction to Paul's injunction was quite negative. I assume that many women have reacted likewise, for a myriad of explanations have been offered to dismiss or explain the perceived unreasonableness of his statement.

To begin, many claim that *lalein* in verse 34 refers only to general talking or idle chatter, and does not include formal lectures, exhortation, or teaching.[1] The implication of this definition would be that women were prohibited from chattering, or disturbing the meeting, but not prohibited from formal public teaching or leading. Hence, these verses "do not prohibit a ministry for women in the church but simply assert that Christian meeting should be orderly."[2]

Lalein, however, is the broadest word in all the Greek language for vocal utterance. It covers every form of address. To prophesy, preach, speak in tongues, teach, command, exhort, admonish, pray — all are *lalein*.[3] The pure definition of *lalein* is ". . . to speak, to employ the organ of utterance, to utter words of any language, independently of any reason why they are uttered, (not to speak inconsiderately or imprudently but) to use the human voice with words — hence, to talk."[4] *Lalein* applies to any form of verbal speech. In the 1 Corinthians 14:34 sense, then, it applied to any open speaking in the synagogue or public place of worship.[5] To assign to *lalein* the meaning "to chatter" in one use in twenty-four in the chapter, when there is nothing to suggest such a meaning in the text, is a desperate exegesis and is not in line with the actual meaning of the word.[6]

Furthermore, this explanation does not answer the contextual demands of the passage. Undoubtedly the Corinthian women were disorderly at times, but if mere order in the meeting (which men are bound to keep as well as women) were all Paul meant, he would not have penned so many long explanatory chapters about the creation of man and woman, the creation of the church, church organization, spiritual gifts, the principle of headship — all to prove that women ought not to chatter in the meeting. As one scholar has commented, this conclusion is just "too little for the bigness of the premises."[7] If Paul were only concerned about order, he probably would have couched the command in more general terms, to include men as well as women. Paul gave specific reasons for the injunction, and chattering was not one of them.

A second explanation offered for the injunction is that men and women sat on separate sides of the room and that the women would interrupt the service by shouting questions across the room to their husbands.[8] This view then goes on to conclude that the command to silence was limited to specific abuses — that is, to questions that women are to reserve for their husbands at home.

Although men and women were separated in Jewish synagogues, there is no documented evidence that this practice was followed in church meetings. D. A. Carson, in *Exegetical Fallacies,* points out that it is unadvisable to interpret Scripture utilizing one's own speculative reconstruction of Christian history.[9] The problem is that we have almost no access to the history of the early church during its first five or six decades apart from the New Testament documents. People who say that the women were calling out questions to their husbands on the other side of the room are giving more weight to their speculation about history than they are to the exegesis of the New Testament documents. In other words, they are saying, "What I think happened in Paul's time is more important than what the Apostle Paul actually taught."

What Paul said is that women are to be silent in church meetings. He either meant it or he did not. If we maintain that he did not, then we put ourselves into the position of being able to call into question any of his writings. We thereby strip Scripture of its authority as the Word of God. Although we may not be comfortable with what the Apostle Paul said, we only have one viable option. We must take what Paul says at face value and compare it to the rest of Biblical teaching on the topic.

BEYOND 1 CORINTHIANS 14

Paul's directives seem to extend beyond the Corinthian situation. He repeats them in his general instructions to Timothy. As in the 1 Corinthians 14 passage, the context has to do with conduct in the body of believers. Paul was writing so that Timothy would *know* how to behave in the household of God (1 Timothy 3:15):

> A woman should learn in quietness and full submission. I do not permit a woman to teach or to have authority over a man; she must be silent. For Adam was formed first, then Eve. And Adam was not the one deceived; it was the woman who was deceived and became a sinner. (1 Timothy 2:11-14)

THE REASONS GIVEN

Paul apparently thought that limiting a woman's verbal participation in the assembly meeting gives visible tribute to the created order and to male headship. He is careful to explain his reasons.

Male, the Firstborn (1 Timothy 2:13)

The first reason Paul gives for the injunction on woman's speech appeals to the order of creation. Paul draws attention to the fact that the male was created first, the "firstborn" of creation.

It is interesting that the order in which male and female were created is appealed to over and over again as rationale for their subsequent roles. Submission in marriage, covering of women in worship, women's verbal participation in worship, and prohibition of woman from the role of elder/teacher all appeal to this chronological and theological fact. Obviously, the order in which God created men and women *was* and *is* significant. Had woman been created first, it is likely that the roles of authority and submission would have been reversed. However, this is not the case.

Paul is frequently labeled a woman-hater, and the prior creation of the male is often called unfair, discriminatory, and sexist. These designations overlook the obvious: *Someone* was created first! At the risk of oversimplification, let me draw an illustration from my own family. I come from a family of six children, yet only one can claim the title firstborn. My eldest brother was *born first*. None of the siblings refute his claim to that title nor to the ensuing responsibilities. They are *his*. He personally did nothing to deserve the title, nor was he especially worthy of it. Rather he inherited it because of his position as firstborn.

In the same way, God endowed His "firstborn," the man, with the responsibility of leadership in the man-woman relationship. For this reason, Paul feels it appropriate that woman respect the man's rights as firstborn (i.e., his responsibility to lead) by limiting her verbal participation in the public assembly of believers.

Difference in Nature — Eve's Deception (1 Timothy 2:14)

The second reason given for limiting of woman's verbal participation in the assembly meeting appeals to the fall of mankind. First Timothy 2:14 points out that Eve was deceived and Adam was not.

Both man and woman were created with different roles and different strengths and weaknesses. Their characteristic weaknesses are highlighted in the Fall. The woman was vulnerable to deception, while the man was vulnerable to disobedience (Romans 5:19). As Stephen Clark points out:

> 1 Timothy 2 does not imply that woman is more defective than man, but that they are defective in different ways. To be truer to the text (since the text is not concerned with defectiveness), we should say that man and woman are different from one another and have different roles in the life of the Christian people and in the plan of salvation as well as different points of vulnerability. Woman functions in complementarity to man. She complemented him in the Fall, to the misfortune of the human race, and she complemented him in the redemption, to the blessing of the human race. The former showed her weakness, the latter her strength.[10]

Thus, in 1 Timothy 2:14, Paul draws our attention to innate differences in the nature of men and women. He is not saying that women are more defective than men, but rather that they are *differ-*

ent from men and that the designated roles for the sexes in the church are also different.

According to the Bible, women are by nature more open or susceptible to spiritual influences than men. Eve was deceived because she was the first to believe the serpent, eagerly desiring the spiritual wisdom of good and evil he offered. Although Eve's situation led to spiritual destruction, in some circumstances, this spiritual sensitivity makes women more open to faith. For example, while woman was the first to believe the serpent, she was also the first non-Jew to believe in redemption. Later on, in the resurrection account, it was the *women* who first saw and were convinced that Christ was alive.[11] Yet another example of this spiritual openness is Mary, in contrast to Zechariah.[12] Both Zechariah and Mary received prophetic messages from angels about miraculous births: Zechariah about the birth of John the Baptist and Mary about the birth of Jesus. Zechariah did not believe and was struck dumb as a result. Mary received the message with faith and submission.

Research in psychology and social psychology bear out the fact that men and women differ in social relating, aptitude, and personality. The evidence also indicates that these differences are not simply a matter of socialization or cultural conditioning.[13] For example, it has been shown that "men have more distance from their emotions, and a greater capacity to detach themselves from immediate reactions, whereas women respond to situations more immediately and spontaneously, and find it harder to distance themselves from the way they feel."[14] In addition, the woman's cognitive emphasis is on intuitive "empathy" or "fusion" and the man's emphasis on personal distancing. In other words, women desire to know an object by drawing closer to it, whereas men tend to distance themselves from an object in order to understand and relate to it more effectively.[15,16]

Women's greater openness to spiritual and emotional influences has also been evidenced throughout history. In the time of the early church, for example, women played a prominent role in the gnostic sect and also in the development of Montanism.[17] Women, more than men, have always clustered around new spiritual movements — a trait we see even today.[18] Although I do not have concrete statistical evidence at hand, in marriage relationships in which only one partner is a Christian, the *woman* usually is the Christian.

Therefore, both psychology and history lend credible support to the Biblical recognition of innate differences between men and women, with a major difference being a heightened spiritual perceptiveness in women. This spiritual openness made Eve vulnerable to deception. She took the fruit because it was "good for fruit and pleasing to the eye, and also *desirable for gaining wisdom.*"[19] Adam, who "distanced" himself from the spiritual appeal of the situation, was not deceived as Eve was. Hence, Paul points to woman's deception as the reason for limiting her speech in the public church meeting.

Although Paul is saying that women are prone to deception, he is NOT saying they are gullible and therefore should not be allowed a forum for their ignorance. To the contrary, he strongly advocates that women teach others within Spirit-given guidelines. For example, in Titus 2:3 he directs older women to teach younger women. In 2 Timothy 1:5 and 3:15 he directs Timothy to follow the teaching of his mother and grandmother. Priscilla, one of Paul's female co-workers instructed a new male believer, Apollos (Acts 18:26). Clearly, Paul respects the intellectual and spiritual capacity of women to pass on God's eternal truth to others.

Perhaps then, Paul is implying that men's greater ability to resist deception makes them more capable of governing the Christian community and of maintaining the teaching of the community. Men would be better able to achieve one of the main purposes of those with governing authority — to provide stability and to protect the community against alien spiritual influences and deception. Hence, since women are more susceptible to deception, and since men are responsible for providing direction for the whole church, women are to be silent in the local church meeting.

Submission in Marriage
(1 Corinthians 11:2; 14:34, 35)
A third reason for woman's limited verbal participation is that the silence of women in the public church meeting respects the marital relationship. Paul is not suggesting that women are to be spiritually apathetic or unquestioning. His statements implicitly assume that

women *will* learn. What he *is* saying is that spiritual leadership in the home is primarily the man's responsibility. The leadership in the local church is also the responsibility of the men. Therefore, women who speak in times of corporate worship are publicly stepping outside of the role God intended for them. In particular, when women ask questions in the church meeting, they *publicly* assume the role of spiritual leadership and/or spiritual guidance for themselves, and consequently, for the family. The offense is *not* that women ask questions, but that they ask them *publicly*, thereby *publicly* usurping the husband's position of spiritual leadership for the family unit.

The practical outworking of this command is as follows: If a woman's husband is mature, she will receive the instruction she needs from him at home and need not ask questions publicly. If her husband is spiritually immature, she should not discourage his spiritual leadership in the home by *publicly* asking questions. Asking *him* at home would encourage him to learn and fulfill his role. If a woman's husband is not a believer, or if he is lacking in spiritual initiative, she should ask other women or ask the elders of the church privately. But she should not speak in the assembly meeting out of respect for the marital hierarchy.

The Created Order (1 Corinthians 14:35)
The fourth reason Paul provides for woman's silence is that her speech in the church assembly meeting "disgraces" the created order. Respect for the created order was to be evidenced in visible and practical ways in the local church meeting: first, by the veiling of women, and second, by women's silence. Paul taught that neglect of this visible tribute disgraced the created order.

Apostolic Authority (1 Corinthians 14:36, 37)
Paul appeals to apostolic authority as the final reason for the injunction against women's speech in the assembly meeting. He reasoned that his own position as an apostle of the Lord Jesus Christ qualified him to make sound judgments on the matter:

> . . . for it is disgraceful for a woman to speak in the church. Did the word of God originate with you? Or are you the only peo-

ple it has reached? If anybody thinks he is a prophet or spiritually gifted, let him acknowledge that what I am writing to you is the Lord's command. . . . (1 Corinthians 14:35b-37)

The Apostle Paul addressed the above verses to the Corinthian church. Earlier, in chapter 11, he corrected them for their neglect of head coverings and their abuse of the Lord's Supper. Then he gave specific instructions regarding gifts and unity in the local body of believers. The section on women speaking in church immediately follows. Paul was most likely correcting an abuse here as well. He effectively closes all dispute on this question by asking the Corinthians a rhetorical question. Did they have more knowledge than he, or could they change his instructions because they exclusively had received God's Word?

Women in the church of Corinth were likely breaking Paul's commands by abandoning head coverings and speaking out. In light of this, we can paraphrase Paul's question as follows: "What gives you the right to change the commands of the Lord that I passed on to you? You Corinthians are not the only ones who have received the gospel, nor do you possess deeper wisdom and insight than I, God's apostle! If you really are spiritual, you will acknowledge that I have passed on God's truth and you will adhere to it!" Clearly, Paul appeals to his apostolic authority as the final and conclusive underpinning of God's plan for limiting women's speech in the church meeting.

The reasons Paul gave for the principle of silence are linked to authority, submission, and the differences between the sexes. These reasons are grounded in the creation and the Fall. Paul unequivocally states that he is passing on the *Lord's* command regarding woman's verbal participation in church. We have only two options in response. First, we believe that Paul was a godly man who intimately knew the will of the Head of the church, Jesus Christ, and that he was telling the truth. Second, we maintain that he was inconsistent, a woman-hater speaking out of his own prejudices. If we accept the latter, we can subsequently question many of Paul's letters. If we accept the former, we cannot dismiss Paul's teaching as irrelevant or inappropriate for us today.

SILENCE — TO WHAT EXTENT?

Practical questions arise if we agree that Paul advocated silence on the part of women in the church meeting. For example, to what extent were his teachings applicable? Were women not to say anything at all? What about women sharing prayer requests? Or reading Scripture? Or singing? And how do we then deal with 1 Corinthians 11 where Paul refers to women praying and prophesying provided their heads are covered?

There are a few possibilities for harmonizing the silence directives with the 1 Corinthians 11 passage. In 1 Corinthians 11, it is obvious that women were praying and prophesying in the assembly meeting, and Paul, in his mention of that fact, does not condemn it. Many feel then that Paul's command was restricted to certain types of speech, namely, speech which provided direction or teaching to the body of believers. To prophesy is to apply truth that has already been revealed, to encourage or admonish.[20] Silence, therefore, did not include praying and prophesying.[21]

The second alternative, is to regard this silence as absolute. In 1 Corinthians 11:5 Paul clearly implied that women could pray and prophesy in public if veiled. Yet in chapter 14, he seems to withdraw that limited permission. Charles Ryrie proposes that we avoid placing the emphasis on the permission of chapter 11 and making chapter 14 and the prohibition in 1 Timothy yield to it. He suggests shifting the emphasis to chapter 14 where Paul directly addresses the topic. The silence of women would then become the general rule and the exercise of prayer and prophesy the exception.[22] This shift in emphasis is justified since the latter two passages (i.e., 1 Corinthians 14 and 1 Timothy 2) are clearly the didactic passages on the subject, while 1 Corinthians 11 only mentions the subject incidentally. Our interpretation of 1 Corinthians 14 and 1 Timothy 2 ought to govern our interpretation of 1 Corinthians 11, and not vice versa.[23]

A look at the time-frame for the writing of these epistles adds weight to this argument. First Corinthians was written *before* 1 Timothy. In the former, Paul was addressing the situation in Corinth at the time. In the latter, he more carefully defines the way the church is to operate. Here he explains the role of women and instructs them to be silent. Thus, when Paul deals with the question of discarding the veil (1 Corinthians 11), he recognizes that some women were accustomed to praying and prophesying in the assembly, but it does not necessarily follow that he approved of it. This important point is often overlooked. When Paul finally does speak his mind on that particular subject in chapter 14, he lays down a strict prohibition against women speaking at all.

Paul was not dealing with the question of a woman praying and prophesying in chapter 11, but rather with the question of a woman's position in the public assembly. It is in chapter 14 that Paul deals with the proper use of spiritual gifts and discusses women's activity in the public assembly.[24] Hence, this second view concludes that the silence of women in the assembly meeting was to be absolute.

Both of the preceding views are feasible, and we cannot conclusively determine which was Paul's intent. Regardless of which position we accept, we must conclude that the verbal participation of women in the assembly meeting was to be limited to some extent out of respect for the created order.

APPLICATION TO SINGLES

We have not yet determined whether Paul's command to silence applied only to married women or to all women. Although in 1 Corinthians 14:35 Paul says that women should ask questions of their own husbands at home, indicating married women, his rationale for the practice extends the application beyond the marital relationship. First, the reasons of the created order as well as the difference in male and female natures apply to *all* women. Second, the Greek word Paul used in these passages has the more general connotation of female rather than the specific connotation of wife.[25] Thus, Paul's silence directives pertain not only to the husband-wife relationship, but also to any woman in a public congregation.[26] Just as in the issue of head coverings, the prohibition has to do with maleness and femaleness, not just with the married state. Single women are obliged to respect the created order just as conscientiously as the married ones.

DOES THIS APPLY TODAY?

Of course, the burning question is the relevance of Paul's instructions for women today. Many elaborate explanations have been pro-

posed to limit their applicability. The most popular theory is that
Paul was prohibiting women from speaking or teaching because
they themselves had not properly been instructed.[27] According to
this explanation, the problem in 1 Timothy was women who
"usurped authority from others, teaching when they had neither gift
nor training."[28] Hence, because twentieth-century women are better
trained and qualified to teach, Paul's directive doesn't apply. His
prohibition was meant to gradually fade away along with the disap-
pearance of social distinctions between men and women.[29]
Following are two examples which present this perspective:

> . . . while Paul *does not actually say it, we may rightly infer*
> that the time will come for women to engage in the teaching
> task of the church once the abuses are corrected and they are
> properly instructed. Can she who bears the Messiah be prohib-
> ited from teaching His gospel?[30]

> . . . we must be careful not to consider this passage the only
> and final word to women . . . this was cultural custom which
> could not be *immediately* overthrown . . . *gradually*, woman's
> intended harmony would be restored by the radical cutting
> edge of the gospel.[31] (italics mine)

But *can* we "rightly infer" that these directives were only relevant for that culture and that they were to evolve until men's and
women's roles in the church and home were identical? No, this presupposition is dangerous. Paul's commands were founded on
unchanging historical facts that have specific theological
significance.[32] The order of creation, the rights of the firstborn, difference in nature of men and women, the marriage relationship, and
apostolic authority are the reasons Paul appealed to for his injunction. He did not cite culture or lack of training, and he nowhere indicated that his teachings would eventually become obsolete. Paul's
reasons are not changed by time, but are authoritative for all times
and cultures. One's own speculative reconstruction of history is not
a valid basis for dismissing his teaching.

Another contemporary theory is that Paul was only concerned
with maintaining the status quo and that he did not want to offend

outsiders. However, this position is also speculative and is without any evidence. First, women often led in the Aphrodite cult in Corinth.[33] Consequently, a woman speaking in public would *not* be shocking to the Corinthians. Second, women prophesied together with men at Pentecost (Acts 2:17-18). The concern for offending others did not hinder their public speech on that occasion, so there is no reason to believe that this concern spurred the Pauline instructions. Third, the "offense" argument appeals to cultural relativism as the basis for dismissing Paul's teaching. Yet, appeal to cultural relativism does not satisfy the claims of the surrounding Biblical text. This is particularly the case in 1 Timothy. James Hurley aptly comments:

> Some argue that 1 Timothy was written to a specific congregation in a specific cultural setting, and that the instructions given are not normative for assemblies in general, nor relevant for another time period. Paul however, deliberately said that he wished Timothy to know "how one ought to conduct himself in God's household." An alternative would be "how people ought to conduct themselves." Paul's abstract language indicates that his instructions should have a general rather than closely limited application. The topics of the letter are not culturally relative, although they could be brought to particular application in Timothy's context.[34]

Hence, limiting Paul's directives to a specific time and culture when the Apostle Paul himself did not so limit them is errant. The appeal to offense and cultural relativism is unfounded.

There is yet a third major opinion, held by many "Biblical feminists" that the Apostle Paul was *WRONG* in his thinking. Paul's thinking was limited by rabbinic traditions and the oral law, and he was inconsistent with what he himself taught in other letters. Dorothy Pape is representative of this group:

> . . . he is literally quoting the oral law . . . this has colored the thinking of most theologians ever since . . . he seems to be clinging to a little of the law, which, according to his argument in Galatians and Romans should have been overcome. . . .

Thus, though he believes in principle that there is no longer Jew and Gentile, male and female in Christ, perhaps for the sake of the gospel he is *accommodating himself* to local thinking. . . .

. . . his teaching is *"rabbinic."* . . . I'm sure that what he wrote *must have been right for that time* [but obviously *not* right for today!]. (comments and italics mine)[35]

However, the above line of thinking is irrational and dangerous. First, Paul's assumption that women can and will learn was *not* a typical rabbinic view.[36] Second, to say that Paul was bound by his rabbinic training in this one area of his thinking is to attack the inspiration and authority of Scripture. What evangelical feminists are essentially proposing is that Paul's personal quirks so affected his writings that we cannot trust his judgment in this matter. If we claim that Paul was bound by his rabbinic training in the area of male-female relationships, then what is to stop us from discounting his teaching on any other matters? Our own human reason would become the judge of what is really God's inspired Word and what is not. We cannot dismiss Paul's teaching in this matter without disclaiming the authority of the Word of God.

The rationale for denying the contemporary relevance of Paul's teachings is not sound. Much as I might like to, I cannot dismiss the implications of Paul's silence directives for present-day practice. The reasons Paul gave for the practice of silence are linked to authority, submission, and differences between the sexes. These reasons are grounded in the creation and the Fall and are not altered by geography or time. The only *sound* conclusion is that Paul's directives regarding the verbal participation of women in assembly meetings *DO* apply today in some way or another. We cannot excuse Paul's teaching on the basis of theological evolution, cultural relevance, or Paul's personal idiosyncrasies.

CONTEMPORARY ACCEPTANCE DIFFICULT

Generally speaking, women today have difficulty accepting such limits. Three major factors are involved. The first factor, which originated at the fall of mankind, is the curse or rebellion of woman

against her designated role. The second factor is the historical mis-
management of Biblical texts. The third is the cultural milieu of
contemporary Western society.

First, women have difficulty with Paul's silence teaching
because they have an innate sin nature which causes them to rebel
against male leadership. The curse of Genesis 3:16 affects their ability to willingly submit to that authority. Subsequently, women rebel
against symbols or actions which pay respect to the authority structure. Submission, veiling, and silence constitute a spiritual
battlefield for women. When the sin nature reigns, rebellion and bitterness against these commands prevail. Only in total yieldedness to
the Holy Spirit are women freed to fulfill their Biblical role and to
experience peace, fulfillment, and contentment within it.

The second contributing factor is "man-made." Historically,
men have abused, oppressed, domineered, and otherwise degraded
women. Unfortunately, Christian men have also been harsh, overbearing, and abusive towards women. And they have used Paul's
teachings to justify their actions. Hence, generations of Christian
women have heard that the Bible supports the superiority of men
and inferiority of women. Women have been degraded and barred
from participation in the ministry of the church based on man's
faulty interpretation and application of truth. It is no wonder then
that women vehemently reject the "oppressiveness" they perceive in
Paul's directives.

For example, one contemporary writer feels that if we adhere
to Paul's rules, we "limit a woman to being a perpetual bench-
warmer, forever learning but never having an opportunity to pass
her knowledge on, a bottomless cup never destined to overflow with
the good news of Christ to others."[37] While men have often thought
Paul advocated benchwarming for women, his teaching actually is
consistent with woman's involvement in active, aggressive ministry.
The above writer rejects Paul's instructions because of a faulty
application of them. Bible truth, specifically the truth regarding gender roles, has been sadly mismanaged.

The final factor which renders acceptance of Paul's teachings
difficult is the cultural milieu of Western society. Feminist ideas
have thoroughly permeated contemporary culture. Any ideology
which even remotely hints at hierarchical structure is vehemently

rejected. Present-day women have been taught to reject authority
and submission without even understanding their proper outworking. Feminism is presented as the ultimate good, and any ideology
which contradicts the feminist view is perceived as the ultimate evil.
It is no wonder that Christian women today have difficulty with
their role. Any woman who seriously adheres to a Biblical principle
of hierarchy is viewed by her contemporaries as deluded or as an
enemy of the "women's cause." The Bible's teaching regarding the
role of women is no longer mainstream. Women who believe and
obey Paul's directives stand isolated in the current of contemporary
thought.

HOW TO APPLY

In order to apply this teaching, believers must first wrestle with the
twofold applicability of silence. If we hold to the view that the
silence enjoined refers only to authoritative teaching or leading, then
we can allow public prayer, prophesying, and sharing by women. If,
however, we maintain that Paul's injunction advocated complete
silence, women today should exercise extreme caution and should
carefully consider whether they need talk in the meeting at all. Both
applications are defendable, yet both have inherent dangers.

The danger in adopting the view that women should be completely silent is that it can become rigid and legalistic and would
embitter and frustrate women. This danger is exaggerated by the
milieu of contemporary society. The danger in allowing women to
pray and prophesy is that contemporary pressure and permissiveness
may expand this practice to include speech outside Biblical limits.
A delicate balance is required between the rigid legalism that has
too often characterized application of the silence directive and the
casual license that seeks to restructure the directive to accommodate
modern trends.

Paul's teaching must be applied with love and tolerance. Those
who hold the view that women are not to speak at all must unconditionally love those women who feel they have more freedom.
Local churches should discuss the issue, but should not be rigid in
applying it. The restrictions on women are not intended to repress,
exploit, or dominate women, nor do they reflect an inferior status.

They simply show a visible respect for the created order. Thus, we must ensure that the directives are not applied in such as way so as to degrade, humiliate, or crush women.

In the past, leaders have self-righteously crushed women's spirit by enforcing silence. The Biblical injunction functions most effectively when internalized by women rather than when externally imposed by men. In other words, women should *feel* free to speak in the assembly meeting, but they should *willingly limit* their own speech out of respect for the created order. They should do this, NOT because of the external rules, but rather because of an inward heart attitude which gladly abides by God's design.

Very few women understand and accept Paul's silence directive, for the issue unfortunately has been blown out of proportion. Women are so bitter about the *limitations* Paul imposed that they fail to see the vastness of the opportunities within the limitations. There are 168 hours in the week available for ministry. Paul is advocating limits to public speaking for one or two of those hours. When put into proper perspective, this limits women 0.05% of the time in any given week. It *is* a sacrifice, yet it is not unbearable, nor is it unreasonable, particularly when observed out of obedience to God and out of respect for His created order. Contrary to the gloomy assessment of Dorothy Pape, Paul's injunction does *not* turn women into "perpetual benchwarmers." They are to be involved in ministry equally as much as men. Ministry opportunities for women are vast. They need to be taught a proper perspective on ministry and on Biblical guidelines for their participation in the local church meeting.

In order to facilitate healthy acceptance of their Biblical role, *women* must be the ones responsible for teaching women their role. This is very much in line with Paul's instructions to Timothy. Paul thought that it was the older women's responsibility to teach the younger women about woman's role.[38] Contemporary women will have difficulty accepting such teaching from men; therefore, it is extremely vital that godly women accept this task.

To summarize, Paul taught that women are to be quiet in the assembly meeting. Yet there may be specific instances in which it is entirely appropriate for women to speak, provided this speaking does not involve teaching or directing in leadership, and providing that the woman respects the created order by means of a head cov-

ering. Because the Pauline instructions are based on eternal principles, they have specific application today. We must agree with Gary
Inrig: "They are *not* the prejudiced remarks of an anti-feminist or a
first-century male chauvinist, nor are they simply the expression of
ancient customs. It is not, therefore, a case of the opinion of Paul, or
of an out-of-date restriction, but of the binding will of the Head of
the Church."[39] The command to silence is difficult for women to
accept because of the Genesis 3:16 curse, because of historical mis-
management of truth, and because of the present-day cultural
milieu. Yet this teaching needs to be applied today as much as it did
in Paul's time. Christian worship involves reestablishing tribute to
the creational pattern by women voluntarily limiting their verbal
participation. In a day when women are speaking out about everything from nuclear war to pornography, Christian women's self-
imposed silence in the church meeting will loudly proclaim tribute
to God's created order.

ELEVEN

OFFICES FOR WOMEN

Laura Sabia, a columnist from the *Toronto Sun*, was interviewed on a recent national news program. In light of the International Decade of Women, she was asked to comment on women's progress during the last ten years. Ms. Sabia stated that the major complaint of women was, and still is, "a lack of power." This problem, she said, is perpetrated by the attitude of women themselves, of men, and especially of churches — churches being very, *VERY* discriminatory as far as women are concerned. According to Ms. Sabia, "women must learn to be aggressive . . . to *know* power! . . . to *love* power!"[1]

"Biblical feminists" would agree with Ms. Sabia. Their goal is for women to have more power in the church and in religious spheres. This power is being pursued on two fronts: first, by women holding offices in decision-making bodies and professional staff roles of national and international religious organizations, and second, by the ordination of women to local church offices such as pastor/elder/bishop and deacon.[2] Jongeward Scott, in *Affirmative Action for Women*, suggests that Christian women initiate political action to change the rules or laws which inhibit the full participation of women in the above areas.[3] She maintains, "uncongenial as overt political activity may seem to many religious women, it is a legitimate and necessary road."[4] Christian women today are being taught that power, or equal position and function with men, is right and just.

Although women's climb to power through ordination to official church leadership positions has become a common trend, this action is not justified by New Testament teaching on the matter. In fact, there are three strong evidences for the *exclusion* of women from leadership offices of the church. These evidences are the direct teaching of Scripture, the indirect teaching of Scripture, and historical precedent. Let us examine these three evidences.

DIRECT TEACHING OF SCRIPTURE
Women Are Prohibited from Teaching and Exercising Authority Over Males (1 Timothy 2:11, 12)

For the purpose of this discussion, I will use the term "elder" to represent elder, overseer, presbyter, bishop, and pastor. As teaching and exercising authority over God's people are the two basic functions of elders, women are disqualified from this role. First Timothy 2:11, 12 states:

> A woman should learn in quietness and full submission. I do not permit a woman to teach or to have authority over a man; she must be silent.

A careful examination of this passage yields two key concepts. The first is the manner of woman's learning — in quietness and full submission. The Greek word used here for quietness means silence, but it also carries with it connotations of peacefulness and restfulness. So when Paul advocated quiet and submissive learning, he was calling for a quiet receptivity and submission to authority.[5]

The description of women's learning parallels the second concept: Women are forbidden from teaching and exercising authority over men. Quiet learning is the opposite of verbal teaching, and full submission is the opposite of exercising authority.[6] The two concepts are thus intertwined and inseparably related.

What is the meaning of the phrase "teaching and exercising authority"? The exercise of authority is significant to the prohibition against teaching; hence, we should look at exercising authority before considering teaching.

Authentein is the Greek word which is translated "to exercise authority" or "to usurp authority." This is the only occurrence of the word in the New Testament. The etymology of *authentein* can convey the notion of exercising authority on one's own account (without authorization) or on one's own terms (arbitrarily or autocratically).[7]

If it means exercise authority, it prohibits all exercise of authority over man by woman. If it means usurp authority, then the passage only forbids women to take authority over men in an improper way. The whole discourse could then simply be a prohibition of wrongful use of authority over men, not a complete prohibition of woman's authority over man. If *authentein* can be translated as usurp authority, the injunction would be limited to bossy, domineering women, or untrained or ungifted women.

Advocates of woman's ordination like to interpret *authentein* in the latter manner. However, there are inherent problems in doing so. First, there is no hint in the passage that the concern is only with *some* women wrongly handling authority. The passage focuses simply on *women*. Thus all women are in view. Furthermore, if Paul's only concern was that authority be exercised properly, he would have written in general terms, since men are just as likely as women to abuse authority. Finally, the parallel directives of the manner of women's learning, of silence, and the prohibition against women teaching clearly indicate that the statement intended to prohibit *all* women from exercising authority over men in the church. Thus, the best translation for the word *authentein* is to exercise authority. In context then the use of this word limits all women from exercising authority over men in the church in the position of elder.

Although many women would agree that exercising authority over men doesn't harmonize with the creational pattern of woman's submission, they have difficulty understanding why women should thus be disallowed from teaching in the church meeting. The difficulty in applying the passage does not arise from confusion in the meaning, but from the difference between the approach to teaching taken by the modern church (and the modern world) and the approach by the early Christians.[8] Teaching today is less a way of exercising authority in a relationship, and more an indoctrination or a transfer of information. But it was not so for the New Testament church. Clark points out that:

We most commonly understand teaching as a transfer of information (facts) or skills. Sometimes we also include values
within the realm of education, but when we think of teaching
values in modern education, we are inclined to conceive the
process as helping students to see that some values are important or attractive. Modern "teaching" does not involve the
exercise of authority over people, except insofar as the teacher
needs to maintain enough discipline to continue teaching.
Modern "teaching" is usually a process whereby an expert is
hired to transmit a skill or information to students who are free
to ignore what is taught. . . . By contrast, the early Christian
understanding of teaching, built upon the Jewish understanding, saw teaching as an activity involving personal direction
and an exercise of authority. The teacher did not just give his
views, he laid out what he expected the student to accept.
Moreover, teaching occurred within a relationship in which the
teacher had authority over the student. The focus of teaching in
the New Testament was upon teaching a way of life and the
truths which underlay that way of life. Students were expected
to follow that way of life, and the teaching was passed on with
authority. (1 Timothy 4:11, 16-5:2)[9]

Women were prohibited from teaching because the *exercise of
authority* was embodied within the New Testament act of teaching
in the assembly meeting.

Although authoritative teaching is unpopular in contemporary
society, it is the type of teaching which occurred in the local church
meeting. Authoritative teaching is rare in contemporary society, not
because it is *wrong*, but because modern man has difficulty submitting. We have been permeated with the philosophy of humanism,
which hails each individual as his/her own ultimate authority. This
philosophy, coupled with an incorrect view of the role and duties of
elders, dilutes the concept of authoritative teaching. However, the
concept is still Biblical and still relevant for today.

To summarize 1 Timothy 2:11, 12, women in the local church
meeting are to learn in quietness and submission. They are prohibited from teaching in the assembly meeting because Biblical teaching involves the exercise of authority over those being taught.

Consequently, this passage directly prohibits women from holding the office of elder with its inherent exercise of authority.

New Testament Churches Were Instructed to Choose *Men* as Elders (1 Timothy 3:1-7; Titus 1:6-9; 1 Peter 5:1-4)

The second direct Scriptural evidence for the exclusion of women from the office of elder is the apostolic instruction to choose *males* for this role. The above passages deal with the qualifications and character requirements of an elder. The passages consistently refer to elders as male. One of the prime characteristics of an elder, the ability to govern his family well, requires an elder to be male. Thus, all Scripture passages which specifically address the matter of recognizing elders within the local church require that elders be men.

Hence, direct Scriptural evidence which prohibits women from teaching and exercising authority over men in the church, as well as apostolic instruction regarding the choosing of men as elders, clearly indicates that this office was restricted to males.

INDIRECT TEACHING OF SCRIPTURE

The evidence for the exclusion of women from the role of elder becomes even more weighty when the indirect teaching of Scripture is taken into account. It is a basic hermeneutic presupposition that the teachings in the Bible are congruous and must be viewed as a whole. Indirect teaching does not specifically address the question of women elders, yet it logically supports the same conclusion the direct teaching does.

The Order in the Church Reflects the Created Order of the Marriage Relationship

The principles of authority and submission are woven into the marital structure. According to Ephesians 5 and 1 Corinthians 11, the headship of men in the marriage relationship is mirrored in the functioning of the church. If one dismisses male headship in the church, he or she is also dismissing it in marriage because they are based on the same principle.[10]

Paul taught that the office of elder was restricted to men. He felt that the created order of male headship in both home and church did not permit women to exercise spiritual oversight of the flock. They could not be in positions of authoritative teaching or exercising discipline over men.[11] The regulations which the Apostle Paul laid down are universally applicable. His commands are grounded, not in time-bound historically and culturally relative arguments that apply only to his day, but in the way God created man and woman to relate to each other as male and female.[12] The principle of male headship in marriage, which is mirrored in the church, indirectly disqualifies a woman from holding the office of elder.

Women's Verbal Participation in the Church Meeting Is Limited

The second evidence which indirectly supports exclusive male eldership is the restriction on women's speaking out in the local church meeting. Paul's command to silence clearly excludes a woman from the position of elder, as one of the functions of elders is teaching and leading the assembly publicly (see 1 Timothy 3:2; 5:17).

Sign of Submission to Be Worn by Women in Assembly Meetings

The third evidence which indirectly supports exclusive male eldership is the teaching regarding head coverings. According to the extensive teaching of 1 Corinthians 11, all women are to wear head coverings in the assembly meeting of the local church when participating verbally. The head covering is a symbol or sign of the submissive position of women in the assembly of believers. Thus, the head covering teaching adds credence to the exclusion of women from any position of governmental authority within the local assembly and hence supports the exclusion of women from the office of elder.

The New Testament Does Not Refer to Female Leaders

The fourth evidence which indirectly supports exclusive male eldership is the absence of any Biblical reference to female leaders. What is *not* said in the Bible can hardly be used as clear teaching, but

when it supports what *is* said, it adds even more weight to the
argument.

There is no mention in the Bible of female apostles, evange-
lists, or elders. Christ Himself did not choose female apostles. His
omission of women is extremely significant. It was not a concession
to the social mores and prejudices of His time, but it was most likely
the direct expression of His view on the matter:

> To argue that Jesus' choice of apostles was determined by cul-
> ture is to ignore that fact that God chose the culture and time
> in which his Son was born. . . . Jesus knowingly overthrew
> custom when he allowed women to follow him. It is uncon-
> vincing to acknowledge that Jesus radically broke custom in
> this regard but conceded to it by not allowing women to preach
> or teach.[13]

Thus, Biblical example, or lack thereof, supports the exclusion
of women from the office of elder.

Evangelical feminists maintain that the Bible does cite examples of a woman apostle and woman elder. Romans 16:7 is the verse
which is quoted as an example of a woman apostle:

> Greet Andronicus and Junias, my relatives who have been in
> prison with me. They are outstanding among the apostles, and
> they were in Christ before I was.

There are a number of strong reasons why this cannot be used
as logical evidence for female apostles. First of all, the New
Testament does not say Junias was a woman. Junias could have
been either a female *or* a male. Second, the grammatical term used
may mean "well-known *as* apostles," or it may mean "well-known
by the apostles." The latter usage is in keeping with exclusive male
apostleship. Third, the term apostle also has general usage. It may
indicate one sent out by a person or body as a representative.[14] A
woman could have easily been sent out as a representative without
holding an official leadership role. Finally, a basic hermeneutical
rule is that unclear passages always yield to clear passages.
Scripture clearly teaches elsewhere that women are prohibited from

offical leadership roles. To use Junias, who may be male or female, as an example of a woman preacher or elder, in the absence of other evidence, is an irresponsible handling of an obscure text.

The second passage used in support of women elders (*presbyteras*) is 1 Timothy 5:1, 2.

> Do not rebuke an older man harshly, but exhort him as if he were your father. Treat younger men as brothers, older women as mothers, and younger women as sisters, with absolute purity.

The term in question refers to older women. The Greek word used is *presbyteras*, which bears striking similarity to the word used elsewhere for male elders (*presbyter*). However, 1 Timothy 5:1, 2 does not refer to the office of elder nor to any office for that matter. Paul is telling Timothy how to behave towards *all* people, young and old, men and women. He is giving Timothy special instructions about how to relate to older people. They deserve respect because of their age even though they are under Timothy's authority. Also, if older man and older women refer to an office, to what do young men and young women refer?[15] Again, the simple hermeneutic rule of the unclear yielding to the clear renders this argument invalid.

Feminists' strained attempts to find Biblical precedent for female elders are erroneous. There *is* no reference to female elders in the Bible, and this fact *does* indirectly support the exclusion of women from the elder role.

HISTORICAL PRECEDENT

The final support for exclusive male eldership is historical precedent. Although not conclusive in itself, historical precedent adds weight to the argument when it reaffirms direct and indirect Scriptural teaching. Scholars have consistently interpreted Scripture as teaching the exclusion of women from the elder role. It is only recently, with the growth of the women's liberation and feminist movement, that this interpretation has been questioned.

For example, in 1951, a council met in Sweden to again examine Scriptural teaching in this regard. All but one of the teachers holding academic positions in New Testament studies in the Swedish universities signed the following statement:

> We, the undersigned, professors and lecturers in the field of New Testament exegesis at our two universities, hereby declare as our definite opinion, based on careful investigation, that ordination of women would be incompatible with New Testament thought and would constitute disobedience to the Holy Scriptures. Both Jesus' choice of apostles and Paul's words concerning the position of women in the congregation have significance of principle, and are independent of circumstances and opinions conditioned by any particular time in history. The current proposal that women should be admitted to priesthood in the Church of Sweden must therefore be said to meet with grave exegetical obstacles.[16]

These Swedish scholars came to the same conclusions as generations of Christians before them. For approximately 1800 years, the Bible was interpreted by scholars as excluding women from the role of elder.

To summarize, Scripture directly prohibits women from teaching and exercising authority over men in the church and clearly states that elders are to be men. The exclusion of women from the elder role is supported indirectly by New Testament teaching regarding the created marital order, women's verbal participation in church meetings, and the "sign" of submission to be worn by women in church meetings. Also there is no reference to female elders in the New Testament. If we base our view on Scripture alone, there can be no other conclusion. In addition, Bible scholars have historically agreed that exclusive male eldership was Scripture's intended teaching. Hence, women are not to occupy the office of elder.

CONTEMPORARY DEPARTURE FROM HISTORICAL PRECEDENT

Although only a few decades have passed since the formulation of the Swedish statement cited above, I would imagine that few

Swedish scholars would now hold to that well-researched position. Current Biblical interpretation has markedly deviated from historical precedent.

Societal pressures have caused this slide. North American society was founded on Judeo-Christian values. These values were generally in line with the teachings of Scripture. In the past, women accepted their role in the church, for it was compatible with cultural ideology. Recently, however, society has moved further and further away from Judeo-Christian principles and values. Current ideologies are based on the religion of this world: humanism. Consequently, people today have difficulty dealing with the traditional role of women, for they no longer possess a Judeo-Christian paradigm. Scripture has not changed. It has simply become unpopular.

This loss of popularity should not surprise us. Christ taught that we would be hated in the world because of our beliefs. In fact, we should expect to be increasingly out of step with modern thought as society strays further from Biblical principles. If our ideology were in vogue, with the ever-increasing corruption in our society, we would have to question the purity of our devotion to Christ and the principles He taught.

Generally speaking, Christendom today is deviating from the precedent of the past by rejecting the Bible's pattern for church leadership. Contemporary theologians imply that the church of today must "mold" its offices to meet the needs of the community. They reason that since women are in leadership positions in secular society, they ought also to hold leadership positions in churches.[17] Unfortunately, this philosophy has been accepted and is now being practically implemented by the majority of denominations.

Rejection of the Biblical pattern of church leadership is not without cost. It leads to compromise of other Biblical truth, since the truth of the Bible is interrelated and in harmony with itself. Thus, if one rejects the teaching on women, one may also reject the teaching on divorce, homosexuality, abortion, and morality. This approach leads to the total accommodation and destruction of Biblical truth. I am not overstating the case, for accommodation in one area of truth always snowballs into accommodation of another. As Francis Schaeffer once said, "Accommodation leads to accommodation —

which leads to accommodation. . . ."[18] The cost of accommodating Biblical truth in the area of church leadership is the eventual compromise of the entire Word of God.

THEOLOGY OF CHURCH ELDERSHIP

A great deal of blame for the rejection of Biblical teaching on exclusive male eldership rests upon the clergy. They have not provided clear teaching on the roles of men and women, and have also been negligent in teaching and implementation in the area of ecclesiology (theology of the church).

Ecclesiology is central to a correct understanding of the role of women in the church. It is because of faulty and/or incomplete teaching in this vital area that many churches struggle with the question of female eldership.

On what basis are elders or church leaders chosen? Generally, churches look at three areas.

Training

The church views elders primarily as managers who get a job done. They are chosen on the basis of their knowledge and expertise in administering and teaching. This knowledge and expertise is usually thought to be acquired by completion of Bible school and/or seminary. The basis for choosing elders is thus *competence* and *training*.

Giftedness

Elders are seen as having certain spiritual gifts or "leadership charisms" required in an elders' group (for example: prophecy, teaching, administration). The primary requirement for selection of elders is thus *giftedness*, or demonstrated competence in exercising one or more charisms.

Representativeness

Elders are seen primarily in terms of how they set direction or mold the way things are done.[19] They are chosen because they *represent* an interest group, a viewpoint, or a certain way of doing things. The primary reason for choosing an elder is thus on the basis of who or what the elder represents.

The areas listed above are all important. Elders in the Christian community *should* be competent, trained, gifted, and representative of the people they lead. However, those who choose elders solely on these bases cannot justify the exclusion of women, for women can be *more* competent, *more* trained, *more* gifted, and *more* representative than men! The important fourth element which is taught in the New Testament, yet which is most often neglected in churches, is that of the elder being the "communal head."

In this view, the elders are the *heads* of a community. They are in a relationship with the people in the community which involves mutual commitment. These leaders must care for the people personally, directing and correcting them as needed. An authority-submission hierarchy is inherent to this relationship — like the hierarchy established in the family unit.

The New Testament teaches that an elder is not to be chosen primarily on the basis of spiritual gifts, but on the basis of his character and his ability to govern his family well (1 Timothy 3:1-7; Titus 1:5-9).[20] Spiritual gifts were by no means irrelevant, but they were secondary to the qualities that enabled a man to take the kind of overall responsibility in the Christian community that he took within his own family.[21]

The leadership in the Christian community reflects the leadership in individual family units. Males are to be the heads. This does not negate women's responsibility in the community or make it less important. It does require that female leadership ability be carried out in the context of the structure of the Christian community. The "communal head" concept places female leadership within the local assembly as subservient to male leadership. This is not because of superior giftedness, training, competence, or representativeness on the part of males; rather, this is simply an expression of the created order. Only when leadership or eldership is viewed in this light can women justifiably be excluded from it.

Men and women would find it far easier to understand and accept their respective roles in the church if they had a proper understanding of church government. Women cannot be excluded from the position of elder (bishop/pastor) without a complete understanding of the Biblical qualifications for and definition of that position. They will continue to rebel against prohibition from this office (and understandably so) unless a clearer, more sound, Biblical model of ecclesiology is presented.

FEMALE DEACONS?

Does the prohibition of women from the role of elder extend to the role of deacon? The Scripture passage that discusses the role of deacons is found in 1 Timothy:

> Deacons, likewise, are to be men worthy of respect, sincere, not indulging in much wine, and not pursuing dishonest gain. They must keep hold of the deep truths of the faith with a clear conscience. They must first be tested; and then if there is nothing against them, let them serve as deacons. *In the same way, their wives [or deaconesses, or women likewise], are to be women worthy of respect, not malicious talkers but temperate and trustworthy in everything.* A deacon must be the husband of but one wife and must manage his children and his household well . . . (1 Timothy 3:8-12)

This is the major passage used to teach that women are allowed to be deacons. The phrase in verse 11 mentioning women (*gunaikas*) seems to imply a new class of persons that somehow relates to male deacons. However, there are many difficulties in interpreting this passage. The term used in the eleventh verse is highly ambiguous. The Greek word that is often translated as wives can just as easily be translated widow, bride, or any adult woman.[22] Therefore, differing views as to the application of these verses have been presented.

Deacons' Wives

A common interpretation of 1 Timothy 3:11 suggests that the passage refers to deacons' wives. Since the context is specifically on male deacons before and after verse 11, having this verse wedged into this discourse seems clearly to indicate that these women are in some way related to those men being discussed. The marriage relationship is mentioned, and the conclusion is that they are deacons' wives.[23]

One objection to this view is that no mention was made of elders' wives in the corresponding discussion of the role of elders in 1 Timothy 3:1ff. Surely Paul would have mentioned qualifications for elders' wives as well, not just for the wives of deacons. It could be countered, however, that deacons' wives could assist their husbands in actually carrying out their ministry while the elders' wives could not. The wife of an elder would be strictly prohibited (1 Timothy 2:12) from assisting in the teaching and ruling functions of her husband.

Another objection to interpreting the phrase as referring to wives is that a deacon's family (including his wife) is dealt with specifically in verse 12. The flow of the discussion thus seems rather disjointed when the word is interpreted in this way. The question which arises is why the discourse would be interrupted in the middle in order to address the wives of the deacons.

Even though an argument can be presented against interpreting 1 Timothy 3:11 to mean deacons' wives, it remains a tenable thesis.

Deacons or Deaconesses

A second view is that this passage refers to an official group of women deacons.[24] One of the strongest arguments for this view is the context of the passage itself. Paul is dealing with the subject of church offices and here has clearly marked out three distinct groups to represent the church.[25] In addition to the grammatical evidence, the example of Phoebe in Romans 16:1 is often cited as support of this view: "I commend to you our sister Phoebe, a servant [or deaconess] of the church in Cenchreae."

Interpreting *gunaikas* as deacon is popular, but there are certain difficulties with doing so. First, if this is indeed a full-fledged office, why is it inserted into the discussion of male deacons? Why does it not merit a paragraph of its own? Basing a whole office on one verse seems suspect.[26]

Another problem is that the word *diakonos* used in reference to Phoebe, and which is translated deacon, was also used in more general terms to describe service or ministry. *Diakonos* was used with such wide meaning that it included the work of our Lord (Galatians 2:17) and that of governments (Romans 13:4). It is the most general term used for all kinds of ministry.[27] The word *diakovia,* describing service or ministry in a general way, is common in the New Testament (*diakovia* and its derivatives occur thirty-four times).[28] It can refer to waiting on tables (Luke 10:40) or offering financial support (Acts 11:29). The Romans 16 form of *diakonos* used in reference to Phoebe is found twenty-nine times in the New Testament. Thus, if one insists that Phoebe was a deacon, then Jesus, Paul, and Timothy were deacons also. Of course, the rebuttal is that in these cases the usage is in the general sense of servant or minister. One must then question the validity of deeming Romans 16:1 as an exception to this general sense.

Phoebe served in some very special and significant capacity of service in the church, but it cannot be proven that she was a deacon in the offical sense of the term.[29] Yet, the language of verses 1, 2 does suggest that she held some official position.[30] It is likely that she was in Rome in some official capacity, as a designated *diakonos* of the church at Cenchrea. Whether it was as a servant or serving officer, we cannot say. Paul's wording simply does not resolve the matter.[31] Phoebe's activity was important to this small church, and certainly her importance and influence are not to be disparaged in any way; but to see in her evidence for an established order of deacons or for female officials in the church may be to see more than the evidence warrants.[32]

Women's subordination in the church is *not* incompatible with the function of deacons (to do works of service), but an isolated case of one female deacon is hardly a strong argument for the ordination of women as deacons in the church. In addition, the crucial passage identifying the qualifications of deacons (1 Timothy 3:8-13) gives no hint whatever that female deacons are to be appointed.[33]

On the other hand, because women *are* mentioned in the midst of the description of deacons, it seems proper for them to be involved in the ministry of deacons. This office does not require ruling and teaching.[34] Many churches thus appoint women to the office of deaconess (rather than deacon in order to differentiate between male and female outworkings of this office).

The early church felt that it was proper to appoint women to an official role of deaconess. The first recorded description of such a role was in the early third century. These women assisted in burial and baptism of women. They taught women, cared for sick women

at home, visited the sick, and informed the elders about the condi-
tion of the people — that is, of women's needs and concerns.[35]
Thus, the role of deaconess, as described in the third-century
church, in no way violated Paul's injunctions against women teaching and ruling.

Whether the 1 Timothy passage is justifiably interpreted as pro-
moting an office for women is debatable. However, the role of deacon,
as described in the Bible, does not conflict with the injunction against
women teaching and exercising authority over men. Therefore, the thesis which promotes *gunaikas* as deacons is also credible.

Unmarried Assistants

A third view, that interprets *gunaikas* as unmarried assistants, is presented by Robert Lewis. Lewis maintains that the passage refers to
unmarried women who assist the deacons in the service functions of
the church. Since the idea that these women are deacons' wives
seems questionable and since the positioning of verse 11 in the
midst of the discussion on deacons seems to demand some kind of
relationship between these women and the deacons, Lewis offers his
interpretation of unmarried assistant for consideration.[36]

The position would be restricted to *unmarried* women because
of contextual and historical reasons. First, in the context of the
verse, the deacons' responsibilities regarding their families are spot-
lighted, yet no such complementary qualifications are added for
their female helpers. Lewis concludes that the reason is because
they had no need of any; the female helpers were unmarried.
Second, the historical setting of this letter suggests that Paul would
not address the role of married female deacons without carefully
expounding on their responsibilities at home, as he did with male
deacons. Since Paul didn't mention the women's family responsibilities, Lewis concluded that the women were unmarried. Lewis
points out that:

> The backdrop of 1 Timothy seems to indicate that women
> were having difficulty fulfilling their womanly responsibilities
> especially to the home. If the women of verse 11 could be mar-
> ried, surely a great deal of restrictive legislation concerning the
> home needed to be spelled out.[37]

Lewis suggests three additional reasons for the limitation of this office to unmarried women.[38] To begin, the ministry of the married woman was basically centered in the home. This is not to imply that married women performed no service functions in the church. The idea here is that her church involvement is to be worked around her ministry in her home, which is an extension of that church. Also, a married woman would not be able to meet the demands of this official service position. Her duties at home would deny her the availability and/or flexibility needed to do a credible job. Finally, Lewis suggests that this is meant to be an outlet for ministry of the most neglected individuals in the church — unmarried females. An unmarried female would be able to give her undivided attention to the service of the church.

Thus, this explanation for the women of 1 Timothy 3:11 is that they are unmarried women committed unconditionally to the service of the church and who, possessing certain character qualities, have been enlisted to aid the deacons in the outworking of their office.[39] Lewis's sound rationale makes his thesis tenable as well.

In examining the three views, we see that 1 Timothy 3:11 refers to women assisting in the work of deacons in some way, although a formal deacon role for women may not have been intended. However, the activities of deacons, as expressed in Scripture, are compatible with the Scriptural role of women. In summary, women are *probably* not to hold the office of deacon, although some flexibility can be allowed for them doing so.

CONTEMPORARY APPLICATION

A healthy, holistic perspective is needed in order to implement Biblical directives in contemporary society. To begin, Christians must understand that the restrictions placed on women are not because of inferior worth, intellect, or ability, but simply because the leadership in the local church is to reflect the order God instituted at creation.

Second, Christians today must have a correct view of justice. In contemporary society, justice is whatever seems right or fair to the individual. But Christians must understand that justice is defined by God's Word and *not* by human reason.[40] Though identical part-

nership of the sexes in the church has greater appeal to human reason and is more compatible with current ideology, exclusive male
eldership is fair and just because it is ordered by God.

Third, male headship in the church is to work much the same
way as in marriage. For example, the husband's headship in marriage neither relieves the wife of responsibility nor requires her to be
passive. It does not make her a simple servant in the house. Instead,
the wife's subordination to the husband expresses an order of
authority with the wife's ruling function carried out subordinate to
her husband's.[41] In the same way, male headship in the church neither relieves women of responsibility, renders them passive, nor
restricts them to works of service only. Instead, women's subordination in the church expresses an order of authority with their leadership and ruling functions carried out subordinate to the males'.

A Biblical hierarchical structure requires certain personal character qualities. Male leadership in the church, as in marriage, must
be enacted with much love, sacrifice, and sensitivity. Elders must be
men who manage their own marriages well in order to have the
character qualifications to lead the female members of the local
church without repression, exploitation, or domination. Thus, male
leadership in the church must be executed with the type of sacrificial
love required in a hierarchical marriage relationship.

Finally, in order to implement exclusive male eldership in the
local church today, personal ministry and giftedness must be rein-
stated. God's Word does not forbid the expression of women's gifts.
Women possess gifts of teaching and leadership. These particular
gifts are not to be expressed within the role of elder, but they should
be exercised to the woman's fullest capacity. Females possessing
gifts of teaching and leadership have often been hurt and degraded
by insensitive males, but that is not Scripture's intent. God wants
women to develop and utilize their gifts to the fullest. Exclusive
male eldership must be implemented alongside the exercise of
women's spiritual gifts.

Implementing the Biblical role of women in the church is
difficult in contemporary society; however, if that implementation
holistically applies *all* of Scripture's teaching, it *is* possible. For
example, in order for exclusive male eldership to exist in the local
church without repression, exploitation, and degradation of women,

proper ecclesiology must exist. In addition, elders must be chosen for Christlike character traits of love, servanthood, and sensitivity in the governance of their own family unit, and not solely on the basis of their education, giftedness, or representativeness. Thus, the correct implementation of the role of women requires the correct structure and function of the local church. Radical renovation in many churches may be necessary to ensure full dignity, equality, and participation of women.

SUMMARY

Thus far, we have established that God wants Christian women and men to publicly and practically show homage to His created order. In marriage this is shown by the husband's loving headship and the wife's submission. In the church, it is evidenced by exclusive male eldership as well as the limited verbal participation and veiling of women in the public meeting. These New Testament teachings regarding male/female roles form an intricate network or pattern. They are based on the Old Testament account of creation and are indivisibly associated with each other and with much other New Testament teaching. Therefore, no aspect of New Testament gender roles can be disclaimed or omitted without injury to the continuity and harmony of Biblical teaching.

In light of this, the insistence by Biblical feminists that women claim more power in the church by having identical function and position as males mocks the authority of the Word of God and dangerously induces compromise of Biblical truth. According to the Bible, women are not allowed to hold the official position of elder, and they may also be restricted from the office of deacon. (The fallacy of Biblical feminist theology will be dealt with in the following chapter.) Thus, contrary to the claims of the feminists, women do *not* need more power in the church. The power in the church must not be possessed by either male or female, but rather by the rightful owner — the Lord Jesus Christ.

TWELVE

FEMINISM

In 1984, a New York church displayed a crucifix which depicted Christ as a woman, complete with breasts, hips, and vagina. Although many believers were disgusted, the statue reflected an underlying ideological current that has profoundly flowed into the religious sphere. An examination of the Biblical role of women would not be complete without an analysis of the feminist movement and its influence on Christian women.

Because women internalize feminism to varying degrees, it's hard to describe the typical feminist. Due to this diversity and to the validity of some of their issues, we can't just dismiss the feminists.

Core feminist philosophy is destructive to men, to the family, and to women themselves. Yet the peripheral concerns of the feminist movement are entirely valid and need to be addressed by society as a whole. These concerns include the dignity and full worth of females, and respect of women as whole persons, as well as specific issues such as rape and wife battering. It will be helpful to classify feminists on a scale as to their acceptance of core feminist philosophy. I shall call women at the core "radical feminists" and those at the periphery "relational feminists."

The ideology of relational feminists is loosely defined. These women are concerned that mutual respect exist in the male-female relationship. They simply desire that women be recognized as whole, valuable persons. Relational feminists react violently against

"Archie Bunker" types who carelessly malign and categorize women's potential and contribution to society. Relational feminists support *attitudinal* change, but do not necessarily support core feminist ideology and are rarely involved in feminist groups.

On the other end of the spectrum are the radical feminists who seek *structural* change in society. Viewing history as a massive plot against women, they want to disassemble any relationship or institution which inherently favors men. Radical feminists advocate inclusive language, lesbian relationships in lieu of heterosexual marriage, legalized abortion, and government restructure of society via affirmative action programs. In contrast to the relational feminists, radical feminists attempt to force their views on all women through influencing legislation.

Within the spectrum of feminist ideology, one can also find a strong vein of spirituality. As in the movement at large, the spiritual aspect of feminism falls along a continuum of ideology which is accepted to varying degrees by individuals. For the purpose of discussion, I will classify the spiritual feminists also.

On one end of the spectrum are relational spiritual feminists who wish to see attitudinal change as to woman's worth and contribution to the church. Further along the scale we see "Biblical feminists" (I do not believe them to be Biblical, but this is how they refer to themselves). Biblical feminists appeal to a new hermeneutic for disclaiming certain Bible passages. Finally, at the core of spiritual feminism are the radicals who have totally rejected the Father-God teaching of the Bible in lieu of a female goddess.

Feminists identify some valid problems in the roles of men and women in the church. All Christians should have a concern for the Biblical equality, worth, and dignity of women. Women's spiritual gifts should not be neglected or suppressed. Relational spiritual feminists oppose the oppression and degradation of women in the local church. They are concerned that men treat women as co-heirs to the gospel. They are one step over a valid concern for equality, however, for they are bitter. This bitterness can drive women toward an ever-increasing acceptance of core feminist philosophy.

Although the presence of embittered feminists in the church is not ideal, the problem can be dealt with. Bitterness is an attitudinal sin that does not directly challenge church doctrine. The problem arises further down the scale at Biblical feminism where the truth of the Bible is skewed to accommodate feminist thought.

Biblical feminists disclaim Bible passages which promote hierarchical structure in the church and in the home. They oppose gender-specific submission in marriage as well as exclusive male eldership. This group of feminists is by far the largest category represented in the church today. Since Biblical feminism logically extends into the radical spiritual feminist position, I will briefly review Biblical feminist presuppositional theology before commenting on radical spiritual feminism.

Biblical feminists do not use traditional logic in their interpretation of Scripture. They have formulated a unique system to analyze the text in order to make the Bible more compatible with feminist thinking. The new hermeneutics contains assumptions which parallel liberation theology, for a basic premise is that women have been oppressed by males and that the true message of the Bible has been obstructed by its male authorship.[1] Biblical feminists treat the Bible as a "human work and not as a fetish," and they "deny divine inspiration to the negative Biblical statements about women."[2]

Elizabeth Cady Stanton, a forerunner of the feminist movement, has presented two critical insights for a feminist hermeneutic: 1) The Bible is not a neutral book, but a political weapon against women's struggle for liberation. 2) This is so because the Bible bears the imprint of men who never saw or talked with God.[3]

Feminists will reject a Bible passage on the basis of its "androcentricity," or male-centeredness. They say that the Bible cannot be interpreted in a regular fashion because of its male authorship. It can only be interpreted properly by bringing it into line with feminist thought. Elisabeth Fiorenza is representative of this opinion:

> I would therefore suggest that the revelatory canon for theological evaluation of Biblical androcentric traditions and their subsequent interpretations *cannot be derived from the Bible itself* but can only be formulated in and through women's struggle for liberation from all patriarchal oppression.[4] (italics mine)

Biblical feminism encourages a "consciousness raising" in order to enable women to see the Bible and tradition with different "glasses."[5] Biblical feminists invent rationalizations to explain away Bible passages with which they are unhappy. They do not seek to understand what the passage is saying, but rather to interpret it according to their understanding of what it *should* say. These feminists call their method of interpretation "higher criticism," which could just as easily be called "reading between the lines."

Rather than understand the text as an adequate reflection of the reality about which it speaks, *we must search for clues and allusions that indicate the reality about which the text is silent.* . . . Such a feminist critical method could be likened to the work of a detective insofar as it does not rely solely on historical "facts" nor invents its evidence, but is engaged in an *imaginative reconstruction* of historical reality.[6] (italics mine)

In other words, the Biblical feminist ascribes greater merit to her *own* experience and opinion than to the text itself.

This hermeneutic is dangerous, for it caters to the idea that humans are their own god, that woman is her own reality. And if we explore the remaining continuum of spiritual feminism, we see that this is, in fact, the logical extension of Biblical feminist theology.

At the core of spiritual feminist theology, the radicals have discarded Father-God imagery taught in the the Bible and have adopted a *goddess* as the symbol of *women's* power, freedom, and independence.[7] They justify this action by saying that the male authorship and prophetic tradition of the Bible had eliminated the "divine female symbol" of goddess which they worship.[8]

The simplest and most basic meaning of the symbol of Goddess is the acknowledgment of the legitimacy of female power as a beneficent and independent power. A woman who echoes Ntosake Shange's dramatic statement, "I found God in myself and I loved her fiercely" is saying "Female power is strong and creative." She is saying that the divine principle, the saving and sustaining power, is in herself, that she will no longer look to men or male figures as saviors.[9]

To the radical spiritual feminists, *woman* is God. In fact, what this type of spiritual feminism is saying is: "I AM A WOMAN AND I AM GOD." Practical implementation of radical spiritual feminist philosophy bears this out, for at the Boston conference on women's spirituality held in 1976, women were even taught how to worship themselves:

> Each woman is encouraged to keep a small *altar* in her home to be used for meditation and for focusing her will. At the Boston conference, women were advised to use *mirrors* on their altars to represent the Goddess. That way, they would be continually reminded that *they* were the Goddess and that *they* had divine beauty, power and dignity.[10] (italics mine)

While relational spiritual feminism may have some validity, total rejection of God's truth is at its core. The true impetus behind the spiritual feminist movement is *not* the spirit of the New Testament but rather the spirit of this present age.[11]

A CLOSER LOOK AT BIBLICAL FEMINISM

Radical spiritual feminism promotes self as God. It is thus totally incompatible with Biblical Christianity. Unfortunately, the underlying motivation of Biblical feminism is the same, radical, self-god philosophy. Biblical feminism is not Biblical at all, and it should have no place today in any New Testament church.

I do not make the above statement rashly or lightly, for Biblical feminism is so pervasive in evangelical churches that it would be foolish to glibly dismiss it without exposing the deficiency in its theology. Biblical feminist theology cannot be accepted, for it is based on faulty presuppositions, incorrect hermeneutics, cultural relativism, and illogical thinking.

Faulty Presuppositions

Biblical feminist theology is established on a foundation of faulty presuppositions which include a synthetic system of logic, as well as a defective view of the inspiration, inerrancy, and unity of Scripture.

Synthetic System of Logic

Biblical feminists have as a basic premise the idea that truth is relative; there is no absolute right or wrong and no ultimate standard. According to Biblical feminists, even the truth in the Bible is subject to alteration. This attitude is well-disguised; however, if one examines Biblical feminist literature closely, one can find numerous examples of it.

> Feminist theology therefore challenges Biblical theological scholarship to develop a paradigm for Biblical revelation that does not understand the New Testament as an archetype but as a prototype. Both archetype and prototype denote original models. However, an archetype is an ideal form that establishes an unchanging timeless pattern, whereas a *prototype is not a binding timeless pattern or principle.* A prototype, therefore, is critically *open to the possibility of its own transformation.*[12] (italics mine)

In other words, Biblical feminists view the Bible as open to alteration. One of the basic presuppositions of Biblical feminist theology is that the Bible is not absolute and that its meaning can "evolve" and "transform." Since the Bible presents no *absolute* standard of right and wrong, feminists maintain that they must decide this for themselves. This basic premise allows them to interpret the Bible in *any manner* appropriate to their immediate circumstances.

It is obvious that a synthetic system of logic ultimately permits *anything.* Biblical feminists are today demanding role obliteration within the church. Tomorrow they will demand the ordination of lesbians. And, who knows, next week we may be asked to accept incest.

Anything and everything is justifiable with this presupposition. Therefore, Biblical feminist adherence to such a presupposition is ultimately at odds with God's absolute standard.

Inspiration of Scripture

Whereas Christians have traditionally believed that ALL Scripture is inspired by God, Biblical feminists maintain that only SOME

Scripture is so inspired. The rest is so male-biased, so influenced by the writers' own prejudices, that it is inapplicable.

For instance, it is argued that since Paul received his training under Gamaliel, one of the most famous rabbis, and since he was socialized in a chauvinistic society, it was natural for him to believe in the inferiority of women.[13] This belief influenced his writings about the role of women. According to Biblical feminists, the passages in which Paul addresses the role of women were not inspired by God but by Paul's prejudice.[14]

The difficulty with this view of inspiration is that *any* disagreeable passage may be similarly dismissed. We could just as easily say that Paul was expressing his own viewpoints when he spoke of sexual morality or doctrine. All Scripture would thus be subject to dismissal as uninspired and inapplicable purely on the basis of our own judgment. Biblical feminists are errant in their presupposition that limits inspiration of Scripture.

Inerrancy of Scripture
Thirdly, Biblical feminists often approach their study of the Bible with the presupposition that there are errors in it. When they encounter passages with which they disagree, they label them inauthentic and/or incorrect. However, belief in inerrancy[15] (absence of error in Scripture) is crucial, or we cannot rely on what the Bible says about the nature of man, interpersonal and family relationships, sexual lifestyles, the will and emotions, and a host of other issues. An errant Scripture would only be a reflection of ancient philosophy and psychology, with little to offer us. Also, as church history has repeatedly shown, groups who begin questioning the validity of small details of Scripture eventually question larger doctrines as well.[16]

Those who reject inerrancy are playing god, for *they* determine which part of Scripture is correct and which is not. The Biblical feminist's presupposition regarding error in Scripture seriously threatens the authority of the Word of God.

Unity of Scripture
Finally, Biblical feminists do not believe that the Bible is unified in its message. Instead, they think that Biblical passages and authors contradict each other. Biblical feminists feel justified in quoting

Scripture to argue *against* Scripture. For instance, they cite "in Christ there is no male and female" (Galatians 3:28) to discount the teaching on role distinctions.

When feminists find an apparent discrepancy between two or more texts, they automatically decide that one or both contain errors. Yet if they were to begin with the presupposition that Scripture does *not* contain errors and that Scripture does *not* contra- dict itself, they would be motivated to find exegetically valid ways of resolving any seeming discrepancy.[17] And it is entirely possible to resolve apparent discrepancies without writing off Scripture as errant and contradictory.

The Scripture regarding the role of women in the home and church is unified in its message and is harmonious with all other Scripture; yet Biblical feminists refuse to see its unity. The unified message of Scripture regarding the role of women is one the Biblical feminists do not want to hear. Biblical feminist theology has a low view of the unity of Scripture as a basic presupposition.

The presuppositions or preconceived notions one brings to study of the Bible obviously affects the validity of one's interpretation. Biblical feminists enter their study of Scripture with faulty presuppo- sitions, which include a synthetic system of logic, as well as a marred view of the inspiration, inerrancy, and unity of Scripture. These pre- suppositions have led Biblical feminists to many invalid conclusions.

Improper Hermeneutics
The second major area in which Biblical feminists err is in their hermeneutical process. Biblical feminists refuse to follow the accepted system of grammatical analysis in their study of Scripture. Traditional analysis holds that the text *says* what it *says* and *means* what it says. It is up to the interpreter to ascertain exactly what the text *says* and derive its intended meaning from that alone. The accepted system is composed of basic rules, or hermeneutics, which assist the reader in determining the author's intended message. Here are some of the basic hermeneutic rules feminists violate.

Context Determines Meaning.
Context in its broadest sense refers to the entire historical and liter- ary setting in which the author wrote. The narrower use of the term

refers to the Scripture immediately surrounding the verse in question. Context is determined by examining the purpose of the book, the plan of the book, and the verses in the immediate vicinity.[18]

Biblical feminists are often guilty of taking a verse out of context — examining a verse apart from the text in which it occurs and ascribing a meaning to that verse which has no relation to the surrounding verses. The most glaring example is their misuse of Galatians 3:28. We will examine the meaning of Galatians 3:28 in context later in this chapter.

Unclear Passages Yield to Clear.

Clear passages are used to determine the meaning of unclear passages. Unfortunately, Biblical feminists give *unclear* passages (such as those referring to Junias as an apostle/elder) more credence than *clear* passages (such as the one where women are specifically forbidden to exercise authority over a man). Thus, Biblical feminist theology violates this basic hermeneutic principle.

Incidental Passages Yield to Didactic.

Another basic hermeneutic rule states that *verses which mention a topic in passing (incidentally) should not override passages in which the topic is specifically addressed (didactically).*[19]

Again, a good example of Biblical feminists' neglect of this hermeneutic rule is Junias. The verse in which she (he?) is mentioned also uses the term apostle. Yet elsewhere when the subject of church leadership is directly addressed, women are clearly forbidden to hold authority over men. Feminists, however, give more weight to the *incidental* example (which may or may not be valid) than to the *didactic* passage.

The didactic passage must interpret the incidental, not vice versa. Feminists err when they base their theology on incidental rather than didactic passages.

Scripture Interprets Scripture.

Scripture must be compared with itself for light on each passage in order to discover the unity of its teaching.[20] In other words, one does not determine the meaning of a passage independent of the rest of Scripture, as the Bible is the best commentary on itself.

Biblical feminists often violate this principle by citing Scripture *against* Scripture. Instead of allowing Scripture to explain itself, Biblical feminists use Scripture to negate itself. For example, Biblical feminists say that Galatians 3:28 negates 1 Corinthians 11:3. This is a blatant hermeneutical error.

Since Biblical feminists disobey the rules for proper grammatical analysis of the text, one must ultimately question the validity of their theology.

Culturalizing

The third major problem with Biblical feminist theology is their use of *culturalization* in interpreting the Bible. Culturalizing limits the application of a Biblical text to a specific culture or time in history when it actually demands a wider application.[21] Biblical feminists culturalize all Bible texts that they feel are inappropriate in our society. Submission of women in marriage and prohibition of women in the office of elder are so dismissed.

It is true that certain Bible texts only hold application for a specific time and culture, but in order to discern whether principles are transcultural or culture-bound, one must first determine the *reasons* given for the principles. If the reasons given are based on changing culture, then the principles may be changed. But if the reasons are based on unchanging facts, then the principles themselves should *not* be changed. For example, Paul bases his principle of submission of women in marriage on reasons such as the created order and the relationship of Christ to the Church. Since these reasons are *not* culture-bound, it is improper to assign the principle to Paul's time-frame.

On the other hand, some Biblical principles are unchanging although their *specific application* may differ from culture to culture. For instance, Jesus demonstrated that we should have an attitude of humility and willingness to serve one another (Mark 10:42-44) by washing the disciples' feet (John 13:3-16), a familiar custom of the day. We retain the principle, although it is possible that there are other ways to express it more meaningfully in our culture.[22]

Biblical feminists maintain that the prohibition against women elders reflects cultural custom, for it does not appear applicable to our day. Yet Biblical principles cannot be dismissed so lightly.[23]

By carefully using the hermeneutical guidelines outlined in chapter 9, Christians can determine whether Biblical principles are applicable today. Unfortunately, Biblical feminists wrongly dismiss eternal Christian doctrine by labeling it culturally relative. They consider Scripture *inapplicable* simply because it is not currently *popular.* Broadly appealing to cultural relativism in order to ignore unpalatable Scripture is a grave error.

Irrational Logic

The final difficulty in Biblical feminist theology is the irrational logic employed in its arguments. Biblical feminists often make false inferences and applications from their observations, ignoring basic rules of logic. Here are a few examples taken from Biblical feminist literature.

Mutual concern and respect is taught by the Bible; therefore, Christian communities should be characterized by harmonious relationships between men and women so that fully qualified women as well as men are acceptable in all aspects of Christian ministry and church governance.[24]

Further, Paul has said in 1 Corinthians 1:27-29 that "God hath chosen the foolish things of the world to confound the wise; and God hath chosen the weak things of the world to confound the things which are mighty . . . and things which are despised, hath God chosen, yea, and things which are not, to bring to nought things that are: that no flesh should glory in his presence." What has been considered more foolish, weak, despised and unmentionable throughout the ages than woman? Therefore it is possible that God could be consistent with his character and intentions by calling and using women in the service of the gospel (*in ordained ministry roles*).[25]

At first glance, the above statements appear sound, particularly since they appeal to Scripture. Yet when they are carefully examined, one can see that their inferences and applications are not logically consistent with the initial observations. Let's look at the above quotes again:

Mutual concern and respect is taught by the Bible [true obser-
vation]; *therefore*, Christian communities should be characterized by harmonious relationships between men and women
[this inference is probably true, although I'm sure the author
has her own ideas about what harmony entails] *so* that fully
qualified women as well as men are acceptable in all aspects of
Christian ministry and church governance [this application is
false according to other Scripture, and it does not logically follow the original observation].

Further, Paul has said in 1 Corinthians 1:27-29 that "God hath
chosen the foolish things of the world to confound the wise;
and God hath chosen the weak things of the world to confound
the things which are mighty . . . and things which are despised,
hath God chosen, yea, and things which are not, to bring to
nought things that are: that no flesh should glory in his presence" [true observation]. What has been considered more foolish, weak, despised and unmentionable throughout the ages
than woman [perhaps some element of truth here]? *Therefore*
it is possible that God could be consistent with his character
and intentions by calling and using women in the service of the
gospel [application inconsistent with initial observation].

To review, the first author is saying, "Mutual concern and
respect between the sexes is taught in the Bible, therefore women
can be ordained as ministers." The second author feels that women
can be ordained because they have been considered foolish, weak,
despised and unmentionable. Yet ordination of women does not logically follow "mutual concern and respect" or perceived sex stereotyping. Faulty rationale is the basis of much feminist theology. A
corollary of the above arguments would be as follows: "Firemen are
always found at fires; therefore, firemen are responsible for starting
fires!" Such logic is not acceptable in any serious quest for truth.
Biblical feminist theology is based on faulty presuppositions,
incorrect hermeneutics, culturalization, and bad logic. It *should not*
therefore, be accepted by any serious Christian.
In our interpretation of the Bible, we must take the same view
of the Bible that the Bible takes of itself. An exhaustive study of the

154 WOMEN, CREATION, AND THE FALL

inspiration and authority of Scripture is beyond the scope of this book, but since most of the passages feminists have difficulty with were penned by the Apostle Paul, let us look at Paul's view of his own writings. In 1 Corinthians 14:37, 38 Paul maintains that his writings are "the Lord's command," while in 1 Corinthians 7:25 he states that his judgments are trustworthy because of the Lord's mercy to him.

Biblical feminists give their own views more credence than the Apostle Paul's. The problem with their method of interpretation is this: Once the possibility of error or cultural conditioning is accepted, how does one determine what parts or principles of Scripture are of abiding authority and value? Human reason ultimately becomes the judge of what is really God's Word and what is not.

Biblical feminists do not believe that God's Word is true and trustworthy nor that it contains unchanging standards for belief and practice. Instead they consider it a mishmash of information (some of it God's pure Word, and some of it only man's invention, molded by a male-dominated culture), and God has left us on our own to figure out which parts to obey and believe. Human reason becomes the final authority, the judge of Scripture.[26]

Hence, Biblical spiritual feminism, in practical terms, does not have the Yaweh of the Bible as its God. It holds, rather, each individual as her own god. A careful look at feminist theology and method of interpretation reveals the malignant humanistic philosophy at its core. Although the relational aspect of spiritual feminism is valid in some respects, Biblical and radical spiritual feminism do not conform to the spirit of the Bible and should have no place in the Church today.

FEMINISTS AND GALATIANS 3:28

There is neither Jew nor Greek, slave nor free, male nor female, for you are all one in Christ Jesus.

Galatians 3:28 has long been heralded by feminists as the emancipation proclamation for women. One feminist has called Galatians 3:28 the "Magna Carta of humanity."[27] Another has called it the "great charter of Christian equality . . . the key to solving the male/female problem."[28] Since Galatians 3:28 is quoted ad infinitum by feminists as rationale for their theology, we will examine both the context and content of the verse.

Feminists maintain that Galatians 3:28 eliminates all social distinctions between the sexes. It is this vision of egalitarianism in Christ that Biblical feminists claim as the basic and most potent impetus behind their movement.[29] The reason this passage is so all-important to feminists is that it is the only real passage in epistolary literature that lends itself to their desired teaching on the role of women. In fact, one feminist author rejects the authenticity of 1 Corinthians 11:2-6, 1 Timothy 2:8-15, Ephesians 5:22-33, Colossians 3:18, 19, and 1 Corinthians 14:33-36, and concludes that Galatians 3:28 is the *ONLY* direct Pauline statement on the subject of the role of women.[30]

According to the feminists, Galatians 3:28 teaches that God has created in Christ a whole new order of relationships. The hierarchical view of social relationships is a product of the old order stemming from the Fall. Feminists insist that social distinctions between men and woman should no longer exist. Equality to the Biblical feminist means the abolition of all gender-based roles in society, church, and the home.

However, it is not at all certain that Galatians 3 is concerned with the question of the social equality of male and female. Nor is it self-evident that tension exists between this text and the other Pauline teaching on the subject.[31] Let us examine Galatians 3:28 in light of the four hermeneutic rules mentioned earlier.

Context Determines Meaning

Within the context of Galatians chapters 3 to 5, verse 3:28 addresses the question, "Who may become a child of God and on what basis?"[32] The central issue in Galatians 3 and 4 is the role of the law in relation to faith. A strong secondary theme is that Jew and Gentile both come to God on the basis of faith.[33]

The Galatians were obviously trying to reestablish external requirements, in particular the observance of the Old Testament laws, as the basis for joining the Christian church (Galatians 3:3-5). One of the major teachings of the Old Testament was that circumci-

sion was required as a sign of the covenant between the individual
and God. The Galatians were advocating circumcision as an
entrance requirement for the Christian community. This placed a
person under bondage to the law, with ensuing obligations to obey
it entirely (Galatians 5:2-6). Uncircumcised Gentile men would be
required to undergo circumcision, and women would be excluded
from this spiritual privilege.

Therefore, in Galatians, Paul is primarily arguing over the
issue of circumcision and the law and how these relate to the
Christian community.[34] He reasons that under the New Covenant,
the Christian community is based on a union which transcends and
transforms racial, social, and sexual distinctions. He points out that
justification is NOT by obedience to the law and works, but by faith
and grace. Circumcision could not be an entrance requirement for
Christian community. Gentile males, who were normally not circumcised, and women, who cannot be circumcised, can come to
God on the same basis as their circumcised Jewish brothers. The
whole point of the Galatians passage is oneness in Christ. In *context*,
Galatians 3:28 states that the spiritual privileges in the body of
Christ come equally to men and women.

Unity of position and privilege in Christ does not mean unifor-
mity of practice nor the obliteration of all differences between the
sexes. Paul does not imply that distinctions of various sorts (social,
racial, sexual, functional) should not exist in Christ. The very fact
that Paul speaks in terms of these distinctions means he recognizes
quite well that they exist. "He wishes not to obliterate them but to
orient them properly in light of and as a secondary reality to the service of the one person unity in Christ."[35] Feminists err when they
use this verse to argue that men and women are being reunited into
a singular male-female identity. Paul was not reflecting upon rela-
tions within the body of Christ. He was thinking about the basis of
membership in the body of Christ.[36] It is an error to use this verse
out of context to prove that all social distinctions are erased in
Christ.

Unclear Passages Yield to Clear

Galatians chapter 3 does not clearly address the question of role distinctions between male and female. Yet there are other passages in

the Bible where the relationship between men and women *is* clearly addressed. Galatians 3:28, which is at best "fuzzy" in terms of addressing social roles, must be *subordinate* to clear passages which teach the submission of wives to husbands and the prohibition of women to the office of elder. To view the Galatians 3:28 verse, which is unclear about social roles, as holding greater weight than those passages which clearly address the topic is a hermeneutic error.

Incidental Passages Yield to Didactic

Passages in which topics are mentioned in passing (in the case of Galatians 3:28, the relationship of men to women) must be subordinate to passages which directly address the issue at hand. Galatians 3:28 is a theological statement about the fundamental equality of both sexes in their standing before God. How this should be evidenced practically in social relationships cannot be decided solely on this basis, but must be brought together from one's broader understanding of Scripture — an understanding formed by studying passages that *directly* address the role relationship between men and women.

Passages which directly address the role of women advocate a hierarchical relationship between men and women in the marital relationship and in church governance. Therefore, to use Galatians 3:28, an incidental passage, as evidence for the abolition of hierarchical relationships is a severe breech of basic Biblical interpretation.

Scripture Interprets Scripture

This fourth hermeneutic is almost always violated by Biblical feminists. They maintain that Galatians 3:28 is "incongruous"[37] or "at tension with"[38] the Bible passages in which women are taught to submit. Inconsistency, self-contradiction, human error, and cultural conditioning in this regard are viewed by feminists as "facts of Scripture."[39]

Yet in spite of what feminists say, Scripture *can* be brought into harmony when it interprets and explains itself. For instance, Colossians 3:10, 11 and 1 Corinthians 12:13 parallel Galatians 3:28 in both thought and form, although Paul does not mention gender in the parallel passages. In all these passages, however, Paul maintains that all humans are equal and that they can all approach God on the same basis. Galatians 3:28 can also be compared to 1 Peter 3:1-7. In this passage, Peter speaks of the unity of male and female as joint-heirs; yet in this very context he calls for a sex-role differentiation between the spouses. Thus, the equality mentioned in Galatians 3:28 is totally compatible with a Biblical view of hierarchy in relationships presented elsewhere in the Bible.

In summary, feminist interpretation of Galatians 3:28 is not in keeping with standard hermeneutic methodology. The strategy of feminists' has been to change the meaning of the text to be compatible with their understanding of what Galatians 3:28 *should* mean.[40]

Feminists base their conclusions about Galatians 3:28 on a false assumption that equality of persons before God requires interchangeable roles. The Bible does not teach, nor does it even imply role interchangeability as a requisite of equality. As Litfin points out:

> The feminists' strained attempts to reinterpret the hierarchy passages, their elaborate reconstruction of the New Testament cultural setting so as to discard those passages, their insistence on ambivalence, bias, conflict, and error in the Bible are all so transparently unnecessary. One does not need any of this to bring harmony to the teaching of the New Testament on male/female relationships. . . . It is as if one has a puzzle comprised of a few basic pieces, which when fitted together form a clear and coherent pattern. But along comes another who on turning one of the pieces insists that the puzzle does not really fit together at all. Rather, he insists, most of the pieces must now be rejected because they form an unacceptable pattern, and in their place a whole new pattern must be designed which is more compatible with the piece that was twisted from its original position.[41]

Feminists believe that Galatians 3:28 erases distinctions between the sexes. In adhering to this premise, feminists have twisted one verse. Subsequently, they have had to come up with elaborate explanations to disclaim the remainder of Biblical teaching on male-female roles, destroying the unity of Biblical teaching on these roles.

Biblical feminist theology is at odds with the Bible; yet there are many who quietly tolerate feminist views and in practice, if not in principle, view the Biblical teaching on marriage and order in the home and church as quaint anachronisms. For some the accommodation is conscious and intentional; for many more it involves an unreflective acquiescence to the prevailing spirit of the age.[42] Leaders in our churches today have also been guilty of accommodating the truth of God's Word by their silence and ambivalence. It is essential that Christians now take a visible, verbal stand against feminist influence in the church, lest the theology of not-so-Biblical feminism be allowed to subtly infiltrate and destroy further our devotion and obedience to the God of creation.

THIRTEEN

TOWARDS A CONCEPT OF MINISTRY

Some aspects of the Biblical role for women may seem difficult or even restrictive to modern women. However, we want to look at a final and balancing thesis. This balance is the ministry of women in the church. If we were to end our discussion without addressing the scope of women's ministry, the role of women in the local church would appear confiningly shallow. Thus, if I could weigh the chapters in terms of the amount of emphasis they deserve, I would ascribe the most significance to this final chapter. The ministry of women in the church deserves our utmost attention, for the crux of the New Testament message is on women's dynamic participation rather than on the boundaries to that participation.

MINISTRY DEFINED

Although the word *ministry* includes activities ranging from singing to preaching, it is most often used to describe the function of people in "the ministry" — pastors/elders or others who receive financial support from other believers. This word, however, cannot be so narrowly applied. Ministry simply refers to the act of *ministering*, the act of performing service or giving things that are needed. The broader application of the term is the more appropriate one and the one I wish to use as a term of reference.

In the New Testament, the usual Greek word for minister is *diakonos*. Occasionally, the word does refer to an official role (that of deacon — in 1 Timothy 3:8), but it most commonly refers to a servant. Also notable, ministry, or the act of ministering, can be either positive or negative. The Bible tells us that Satan has ministers (2 Corinthians 11:15), and that it is possible to be a "minister to sin" (Galatians 2:17). However, the most common usage of the word is positive, referring specifically to service within the Christian context.

A minister, therefore, is anyone who serves others. Christian ministry in the New Testament is not the exclusive privilege of an official or priestly caste, but it is for everyone. I am a minister. You are a minister. We are ministers to whomever or whatever we serve.

Christian ministry, or service, can be classified into three broad categories: loving service to the needs of humanity at large, mutual service within the fellowship of Christ's body, and finally, the service or ministry of the gospel.

Jesus met the basic needs of humanity. He taught us to minister to the poor, the sick, the destitute, the lonely, and the needy with compassion (Matthew 25:42-45). Christians, of all people, are to be sensitive to people's needs. Ministry in this first context is practical. Famine relief, counseling alcoholics, homes for unwed mothers, food banks, and medical care are examples of loving service to the needs of humanity.

The second category of ministry is service within the fellowship of Christ's body. It is most frequently rendered *to* the saints *by* the saints. First Peter 4:10 instructs believers to use their respective gifts to serve each other (see also 2 Corinthians 8:4; 9:1; 1 Corinthians 16:15; Hebrews 6:10). Examples of ministry in this category include teaching, encouragement, generosity, serving, faith, and healing.

Finally, there is the ministry of the gospel. This ministry seeks to reconcile the world to Christ. It entails preaching and proclaiming the gospel to the unsaved (1 Peter 1:12). In one sense, every Christian has a ministry of reconciliation (2 Corinthians 5:18), but at the same time, some are particularly enabled in this area.

EVERY Christian has the capacity for ministry in one or more of the above three categories. If you are a believer, you can and should be a minister. The idea that the remunerated workers are the only ones really equipped for ministry has severely damaged the status of women. By limiting ministry to the "professional clergy" and by disallowing women from this role, the church has kept women from the full scope of ministry. This is a crime. God has enabled all of us, both women and men, to serve by His grace (Romans 12:6). He wants all women and men to be ministers. Ministry is for *everyone*.

THE PROBLEMS

Beyond question, the modern church needs more women ministers. To function effectively, the church needs *all* women to fulfill the Biblical directive to minister.

While the Biblical blueprint for ministry is identical for both men and women, it seems that women in particular have been discouraged from ministry in the church. Everywhere I go, I meet women who feel frustrated and repressed by the limitations placed upon them. While the problems that have led to this situation are complicated and interrelated, I believe that they can be divided into three broad categories. The first problem is an incorrect view of the ministry, role, and function of elders. The second and third problems are the neglect of the fundamentals of discipleship and a faulty understanding and application of spiritual giftedness. Each of these categories deserves attention far beyond the limits of this chapter. However, it is necessary to mention them, even though briefly, in order to establish a correct concept of ministry.

Incorrect View of Elders' Ministry, Role, and Function

The major components of this problem are the gap between clergy and laity, the faulty selection process of elders, and the neglect of plurality of elders.

Clergy Versus Laity

Since the time of the New Testament church, a distinction has developed between clergy and laity. This distinction is foreign to the early church's concept of believers and church governance. In the Bible, the laity (Greek, *laikoi*) referred to the *whole* people of God, both those employed in the secular world and those supported by other Christians. Laity was a term of honor since the whole people of God in Christ were chosen to be a "royal priesthood, a holy nation, a people (*laikoi*) belonging to God" (1 Peter 2:9).[1] *All* were God's people. *All* were called to be ministers. *All* were priests. From the beginning, Christianity was essentially a lay movement, and it was a long time before the term lay meant second-class status.[2]

The distinction between professional and nonprofessional developed for three major reasons. First, the Old Testament model of priestly leadership was wrongly projected into the New Testament church. Second, a growing sacramentalism demanded that a special person, the priest, dispense the sacraments, while the laity were the passive recipients.[3] The final influence was the increasing secularization of the church. As Paul Stevens points out:

> . . . the most pernicious influence in the decline of the laity is still with us: secularization by copying the world's leadership patterns. In the Greco-Roman world the municipal administration had two parts: the *klêros* (clergy), the magistrate and the *laos* (layperson), the ignorant and uneducated citizen. The same defamatory distinction prevails today when people argue for secular management structures in church organization. . . .[4]

Even a light reading of the New Testament clearly reveals that church leaders do not receive a special "calling," for ALL believers are called by God to minister. Church leaders *do* fulfill their call in a unique way, providing direction for a local assembly of believers. Yet, in terms of their call, or status, they are no different from any other believer. They are merely laity enabled by God to provide a specific type of leadership for other laity. Thus, the distinction that has evolved between the "professional clergy" and laity is artificial. In God's eyes, all believers are laity, and all believers are clergy. There is no distinction.

This clergy/laity distinction has contributed to the inferior status of women. The clergy are considered experts, while the laity are the passive recipients of the clergy's expertise in terms of knowledge, giftedness, and ministry. Forbidding women to become clergy has reinforced their passive role. While men were able to join the clergy elite and pursue that ministry outlet, women were destined to remain untrained, ungifted, and uninvolved. Clearly, the traditional role model of the professional Christian has dissuaded women from pursuing active ministry.

Faulty Elder Selection Process

The vast majority of churches choose or hire elders on the basis of their training or level of education, their giftedness, or their representativeness. In doing so and in restricting women from this role, churches are nonverbally communicating that women are somehow less capable, less intelligent, less gifted, and less representative than men.

In the New Testament, elders were chosen primarily on the basis of their character and their ability to govern their families well. Women were not selected as leaders because the role of an elder was to reflect the order God established at creation. It is important to note that the exclusion of women was *not* because of any inherent inferiority or lack of academic ability or skill.

Today elders/pastors are commonly hired from outside the local church body. They are chosen because of their level of education or their past performance or because they represent a certain denominational viewpoint. Rarely is an elder chosen from within the congregation because of the congregation's familiarity with his personal character and his leadership in his home. Hence, today's selection process is far removed from that of the early church. The nonverbal message communicated when women are forbidden from the pulpit and when elders are chosen on this faulty basis is that women are inferior and less capable of ministry. This contributes to the frustration and lack of ministry involvement of women.

Neglect of Plurality

Today professional leaders are hired to do a job. Most churches can afford to financially support only one man, and this man is expected to administer, lead, teach, equip, and evangelize on behalf of the entire body of believers. While the neglect of plurality has put undue and unbiblical pressure on solo leaders, it has also discouraged anyone else from exercising and developing spiritual gifts. The

New Testament does not support our contemporary "one-man show." Leadership, in a Biblical context, was always carried out by a plurality of godly men.

The neglect of plurality has indirectly contributed to the inferior status of women in the church. It has fostered the idea that the hired "professional clergy" are the most capable of ministering in the church while those who do not earn their livelihood in this manner are unprofessional, unequipped, and incapable of providing quality leadership. Therefore, women, who do not have the option of pursuing the clergy role arc classified as amateurs.

To summarize, the incorrect perception of the ministry, role, and function of elders has greatly contributed to the discouragement of women's ministry. Remunerated believers (pastors) have been singled out and assigned extrabiblical status, and unpaid believers have been relegated to a lesser ministry status or role. Since women have been disallowed from occupying the role of pastor (elder), they have been discouraged from developing personal ministry.

Neglect of Principles of Discipleship

The second major problem which has contributed to an inferior ministry status for women is a neglect of the fundamental principles of discipleship. Discipleship, or the equipping of the saints, is perceived as the duty of the elders or leaders of the church. This should not be.

Biblical discipleship involves a commitment to pursue personal godliness and to train others in godliness. It is by far the largest area of ministry — to which *all* believers are called. Assigning this responsibility to the "professional clergy" has stripped the majority of God's people of their responsibility and calling.

In addition, the process of discipleship is wrongly viewed as the imparting of information. Believing discipleship to be accomplished through a set educational program, believers do not feel any responsibility to be involved.

Neglect of the discipleship process has markedly affected the ministry of women in the church. Viewing discipleship as a mere program and delegating that program to the professional has excluded women from a large, vital area of ministry.

Misunderstanding of Spiritual Gifts

While most would agree that all believers are endowed with spiritual gifts, the evidence suggests that people believe the Spirit gives certain gifts to men and others to women. For example, men have gifts such as teaching, administering, evangelizing, and leading so that they can fulfill their roles as rulers in the body of Christ. On the other hand, women are thought to have the more service-related gifts of helps, mercy, and faith so they can support the men.[5] There is no evidence in the Bible, however, which suggests that gifts are assigned by gender. The Holy Spirit disperses all gifts according to His pleasure.

Women with leadership gifts are often caught in a dilemma. In the traditional church setting, only the "professional clergy" have been allowed to lead, to teach, to evangelize, and to administer. Consequently, women with these gifts have been immensely frustrated. The Spirit has prompted them to exercise their gifts; however, the church structure has provided no outlet for ministry.

This conflict has troubled women for centuries. Joan of Arc was a prime example. No wonder then that women worldwide have resisted the limitations placed on them and have boldly claimed the clergy office for themselves.

Women today have crossed the boundaries set by Scripture in order to find fulfillment in the exercise of their spiritual gifts. While I can understand their frustrations, I am sad to say that this action is not the answer to woman's dilemma. On the contrary, it only leads the church further away from its Biblical purpose and ministry, and does nothing to help ordinary men and women learn to exercise their spiritual gifts.

To summarize, women in the church have been repressed and shut out from the full spectrum of ministry due to three problems: an incorrect view of the role and function of elders and concurrent neglect of the priesthood of believers, a neglect of the fundamentals of discipleship, and a faulty understanding and application of spiritual giftedness. The Biblical role of women in the church cannot be enacted properly while these problems exist. Contemporary history bears out the fact that radical change is needed to remove the barriers to women's ministry.

The church today has two options. Either it will maintain the status quo and keep reinterpreting Scripture to accommodate modern trends, or it will attempt to correct the problems by returning to a Biblical pattern for church governance and function.

THE SOLUTION

Feminism has long complained that women have not been allowed full participation in churches. Although the philosophy behind feminism is wrong, the movement does address a crucial issue. However, the answer does *not* lie in allowing women into "professional clergy" roles. Instead, the church needs to resurrect the Biblical concept of ALL believers being full-time ministers, return to the fundamentals of discipleship, and correctly apply spiritual giftedness.

The Priesthood of Believers

The vast gap between the clergy and laity must be dissolved. *Every* believer must be regarded as equally responsible and equally capable of exercising a spiritual ministry. All types of ministry must be valued equally.

For the "professional clergy," this mandate is a monumental challenge. No other position currently affords more opportunity to teach, encourage, equip, and challenge believers to develop personal vision and take personal responsibility for ministry. These leaders can also teach Christians the truth regarding the priesthood of believers.

For unpaid "nonprofessionals," this mandate requires a determined shift in thinking. *Every* individual must assume responsibility and take personal initiative in ministry. Congregations must corporately reevaluate the expectations and demands they currently place on their leadership.

This mandate is particularly liberating for women, as it reaffirms that they are equal in capacity and responsibility for ministry. Women should pursue this challenge to develop and exercise their own gifts.

The return to the Biblical priesthood or *laikoi* of all believers requires radical change of current thought patterns regarding the clergy and laity. It also requires humble dependence on the Spirit of

God to work in our midst. Above all, it requires understanding and adherence to the Word of God. The priesthood of believers must be restored. Only when this is accomplished will women be restored to equal partnership in the ministry of the church.

A Return to Fundamentals of Discipleship

In Titus 2, Paul instructs older, more spiritually mature Christians to teach immature believers. This book cannot go into the specifics and practicalities of discipleship, but can merely say that discipleship is a challenging, time-consuming, and fulfilling ministry. Women can reclaim much lost ministry by training other women to be disciples. I would urge all women to grasp the concept of discipleship. Pursue it. Read about it. And most of all, DO IT! Discipleship is simple, yet it requires definite steps to make room for it in one's life. It challenges the individual in personal ministry as nothing else can.

Using Spiritual Gifts

It is a great tragedy when local churches do not allow for the development of spiritual gifts of individual members. Equally tragic is the overemphasis on one spiritual gift (teaching or tongues, for example) to the exclusion of others. The Bible teaches that the Holy Spirit has endowed the church with *many* gifts — many *different* kinds of gifts.[6] The ministry of women, and of men for that matter, is thwarted unless the church recognizes, encourages, and allows for the recognition and nurturing of personal spiritual giftedness.

There is no evidence in the Bible that gifts are assigned by gender. While it is true that elders may possess gifts of teaching, administration, and pastoring, it is equally true that women possess these identical gifts. How then does a women with the gift of leadership, pastoring, or teaching exercise that gift outside of the role of elder?

Numerous avenues for ministry can be open for the creative exercise of spiritual leadership gifts. Local churches must recognize this fact and must encourage and nurture the exercise of each woman's individual gift. Elders would be wise to develop strong female leadership in the church and to consult and collaborate with this leadership in guiding, instructing, and nurturing other women in the church.

For full exercise of spiritual gifts, we must abolish the mistaken views of clergy and laity. Clergy are, after all, only laity gifted and commissioned by the Holy Spirit in a particular manner. The abolition of the clergy-laity gap will emancipate believers to develop their own spiritual gifts in service of the body. It will also absolve church leaders from the burden and responsibility of doing it all. Freed from ministry tasks they may not be gifted to perform, elders will be able to develop and exercise their own particular gifts.

Spiritual gifts are essential for the proper functioning of the church; yet many churches fear and oppose the exercise of spiritual gifts. The call to return to New Testament teaching on giftedness is threatening. It requires a revolutionary restructure of current thought and often of church customs and practices. However, unless the church allows for the working of the Holy Spirit in its midst, it will be ineffective in the world, and it will continue to struggle with the question of the ministry of women. Allowing spiritual gifts creates an outlet for the ministry of women. Neglecting outlets for spiritual giftedness fosters rebellion against the New Testament pattern for male church leadership.

TOWARD A CONCEPT OF MINISTRY

I must admit that my concept of women's ministry has greatly changed in the past few years. Initially, I thought only of a program. While programs have their place, the mandate for women's ministry is not carried out in programs.

Traditional women's clubs, missionary societies, and teas meet the needs of a certain type of individual, but not of others. The Biblical mandate for women's ministry is larger than these activities, and it cannot be neatly categorized and defined. It is unique for each individual. Women's ministry can be *served* by a program, but the program is NOT the ministry! Programs will live and die, but the Biblical plan for ministry is timeless. It is *impossible* to implement a program to meet everyone's needs, yet the Biblical plan can meet the needs of *all*.

In conclusion, I feel that an understanding of the Biblical plan for church governance, function, and ministry is requisite for addressing the questions posed by feminism and contemporary society. Today, the church needs to return to its Biblical mandate, and women need to return to the foundation of ministry. Now, more than ever, women need to be disciples, to disciple other women, and to recognize, develop, and utilize their individual spiritual gifts. In this way, women will reclaim lost status and reinstate themselves as ministers together equally with men.

BEYOND THE CURSE

The New Testament teaches the full equality of women within a hierarchical structure. The role of women, as taught in the Bible, is based on the created order and is intimately related to universal principles of authority and submission. Furthermore, the Bible maintains that gender roles reflect Christ's relationship to the Church and to individual believers. Therefore, the rejection of the New Testament pattern for gender roles has ramifications that extend far beyond mere role restructure. Such rejection will eventually lead to moral decay and even to a disregard for all of God's truth.

Historically, the Bible teaching about gender roles has been poorly managed and implemented. Men have often repressed women by confining them to a stereotyped role. Men have thus abused their God-given role of leadership within both the home and church. Consequently, women have been frustrated within a role supposedly Biblical, yet not Biblical at all.

In contemporary Christendom, the "Biblical" feminist movement is attempting to rectify this evil by advocating identical role and function for male and female. Although I agree with their contention that women have wrongly been repressed and barred from ministry in the church, I cannot accept their solution. The solution for historical role abuse lies not in a rejection of Scriptural truth, but rather in a return to the proper implementation of that truth. Biblical directives, when implemented in a godly manner, are never repressive.

True, the Biblical ideals presented in this book are difficult to understand and accept in the cultural milieu of Western society. Particularly difficult are the restrictions on women's role in the public church meeting and church governance. However, I am convinced that the God of the Bible is not interested in repressing women. On the contrary, God's directives for gender roles seek to reinstate the created order of male and female unity and equality. While I must admit that I do not fully understand *why* God's plan involves a difference in the role and function of the sexes, I *am* convinced that God has a perfect perspective on what is good and just. Therefore, I believe that true equality will only result from pure application of *God's* role directives.

Today, monolithic equality and role obliteration are presented as the utopian ideal. The world tells women that equality and liberation will only be achieved by fighting for their *rights*. The Bible message stands in marked contrast to these ideas. The Word of God maintains that it is in relinquishing one's rights that *true* equality is attained. Women are truly liberated, and hence truly fulfilled, only when they overcome the curse of role rebellion and willingly place themselves back into the pattern of God's created order.

NOTES

CHAPTER ONE *The Created Order*

1. From Genesis 1 and 2.
2. Phyllis Trible, "Eve and Adam: Genesis 2-3 Reread," *Andover Newton Quarterly*, 13:4 (March 1973): 251.
3. John E. Hartley, *Theological Wordbook of the Old Testament: Vol. II*, eds. R. Laird Harris, Gleason L. Archer, Jr., and Bruce K. Waltke (Chicago: Moody Press, 1980), 767-768.
4. C. F. Keil and F. Delitzsch, *Biblical Commentary on the Old Testament, Vol. I: The Pentateuch* (Grand Rapids: Wm. B. Eerdmans Publishing Co., 1959), 63; W. Gunther Plaut, *The Torch: A Modern Commentary* (New York: Union of American Hebrew Congregations, 1981), 36.
5. Mernahem M. Kasher, *Encyclopedia of Biblical Interpretation, Genesis: Vol. I* (New York: American Biblical Encyclopedia Society, 1953), 60.
6. Susan T. Foh, *Women and the Word of God* (Phillipsburg, NJ: Presbyterian and Reformed Publishing Co., 1979), 59.
7. Genesis 2:19, 20.
8. Bruce K. Waltke, "The Theology of Genesis," *Bibliotheca Sacra*, October 1975, 341.
9. George Bush, *Notes on Genesis* (Minneapolis, MN: James & Klock Publishing Co., 1860), 66; Keil and Delitzsch, *Biblical Commentary on the Old Testament, Vol. I, 88.*
10. Genesis 1:27.
11. Cross-references: Deuteronomy 33:7; Hosea 13:9; Psalm 70:1, 115:9-11: 121:1-2; 146:5; See also: Clarence J. Vos, *Woman in Old Testament Worship* (Delft: N.V. Verenigde, Druikkerijen Judels & Brinkman, N.D.), 16.
12. Carl Schultz, *Theological Wordbook of the Old Testament: Vol. II*, 661.
13. Foh, *Women and the Word of God*, 60.
14. Francis A. Schaeffer, *Genesis in Space and Time* (Downers Grove, IL: InterVarsity Press, 1972), 47.
15. Ronald B. Allen, *Theological Wordbook of the Old Testament: Vol. II*, 690.
16. Earl S. Kalland, *Theological Wordbook of the Old Testament: Vol. I*, 177-178.

17. Bush, *Notes on Genesis*, 69.
18. Foh, *Women and the Word of God*, 62.

CHAPTER TWO *Born Cursed*

1. Susan T. Foh, *Women and the Word of God* (Phillipsburg, NJ: Presbyterian and Reformed Publishing Co., 1979), 63.
2. V. Geehardus, *Biblical Theology* (Grand Rapids: Wm. B. Eerdmans Publishing Co., 1971), 45.
3. Henri Blocher, *In the Beginning* (Downers Grove, IL: InterVarsity Press, 1984), 139.
4. *Ibid.*
5. *Ibid.*
6. Genesis 3:13; 1 Timothy 2:14.
7. Carl Schultz, *Theological Wordbook of the Old Testament: Vol. II*, eds. R. Laird Harris, Gleason L. Archer, Jr., and Bruce K. Waltke (Chicago: Moody Press, 1980), 656.
8. Aida Besancon Spencer, *Beyond the Curse* (Nashville: Thomas Nelson, 1985), 32.
9. Carl Schultz, *Theological Wordbook of the Old Testament: Vol. II*, 656.
10. Genesis 3:14, 15 is the first prophecy of the coming of Christ — the Messiah who would deliver mankind from the power of sin.
11. Ronald B. Allen, *Theological Wordbook of the Old Testament: Vol. II*, 687.
12. *Ibid.*, 687-688.
13. *Ibid.*, 223, 378.
14. James Carlisle, "Labor's Pain Still Severe — Survey," *Edmonton Journal* (October 14, 1985), Section D.
15. E. Margaret Howe, *Women and Church Leadership* (Grand Rapids: Zondervan Publishing House, 1982), 50-51.
16. Victor Hamilton, *Theological Wordbook of the Old Testament: Vol. I*, 913.
17. *Ibid.*, 534.
18. Henry A. Virkler, *Principles and Processes of Biblical Interpretation* (Grand Rapids: Baker Book House, 1981), 109; J. Robertson McQuilkin, *Understanding and Applying the Bible* (Chicago: Moody Press, 1983), 98.
19. Foh, *Women and the Word of God*, 68.
20. Virkler, *Principles and Processes of Biblical Interpretation*, 107.
21. A. Weiser, *The Old Testament: Its Formation and Development* (New York: Association Press, 1961), 24.
22. George Bush, *Notes on Genesis* (Minneapolis, MN: James & Klock Publishing Co., 1860), 62.
23. Romans 5.
24. *Ibid.*
25. Blocher, *In the Beginning*, 140.
26. Spencer, *Beyond the Curse*, 31.
27. Hebrews 2:14; 8; 9:15; Galatians 1:4; 3:22; 1 John 5:19; Ephesians 6:12; James 1:21; Romans 6; 8; 1 Peter 1:3-5. See also George Eldon Ladd, *The Gospel of the Kingdom* (Grand Rapids: Wm. B. Eerdmans Publishing Co., 1952), 67.

CHAPTER THREE *Authority and Submission*

1. A. Duane Litfin, "Evangelical Feminism: Why Traditionalists Reject It," *Bibliotheca Sacra* 136 (1979): 267.

2. Philippians 2:6-11
3. *The Lexicon Webster Dictionary* (Delair Publishing Co., 1983), 976.
4. G. Delling, *Theological Dictionary of the New Testament, Vol. 8*, ed. Gerhardt Kittel (Grand Rapids: Wm. B. Eerdmans Publishing Co., 1964), 27-48.
5. James B. Hurley, *Man and Woman in Biblical Perspective* (Grand Rapids: Zondervan Publishing House, 1981), 142.
6. Letha Scanzoni and Nancy Hardesty, *All We're Meant to Be* (Waco, TX: Word Books, 1974), 101-111.
7. *Ibid.*, 179.
8. Hurley, *Man and Woman in Biblical Perspective*, 143.
9. *Ibid.*, 144.
10. John 13:34, 35; 15:12, 17; Romans 1:12; 12:5, 10, 16; Romans 14:13, 19; 15:5, 7; 16:16; 1 Corinthians 12:25; Galatians 5:13; 6:2; Ephesians 4:2, 25, 32; 5:21; Philippians 2:3; Colossians 3:9, 13; 4:18; 5:11, 15; Titus 3:3; Hebrews 10:24; James 4:11; 5:9, 16; 1 Peter 4:9; 5:5; 1 John 1:7.
11. Hurley, *Man and Woman in Biblical Perspective*, 147.
12. Authority = *authentein* (Gr.): power (delegated), authority to do anything; permission, license. E. W. Bullinger, *A Critical Lexicon and Concordance to the English and Greek New Testament* (Grand Rapids: Zondervan Publishing House, 1975), 76.
13. John 5:27; 2 Corinthians 10:8; Matthew 8:9
14. Scanzoni and Hardesty, *All We're Meant to Be*, 102.
15. *Ibid.*, 102.
16. Susan T. Foh, *Women and the Word of God* (Phillipsburg, NJ: Presbyterian and Reformed Publishing Co., 1979), 149.
17. Litfin, "Evangelical Feminism," 265-266.
18. Matthew 20:25-28; Mark 10:42-45.
19. Hurley, *Man and Woman in Biblical Perspective*, 148.
20. Litfin, "Evangelical Feminism," 266.
21. John 10:30; 17:11; Philippians 2:6.
22. John 17:2; 1 Corinthians 11:3.
23. Foh, *Women and the Word of God*, 136.
24. Hurley, *Man and Woman in Biblical Perspective*, 161.
25. Paul K. Jewett, *Man as Male and Female* (Grand Rapids: Wm. B. Eerdmans Publishing Co., 1975), 137ff; Scanzoni and Hardesty, *All We're Meant to Be*, 91, 107, 202-205.
26. George W. Knight III, *The New Testament Teaching on the Role Relationship of Men and Women* (Grand Rapids: Baker Book House, 1977), 22.
27. *Ibid.*, 27.
28. Scanzoni and Hardesty, *All We're Meant to Be*, 22; Virginia Ramey Mollenkott, *Women, Men and the Bible* (Nashville: Abingdon, 1977), 114; Don Williams, *The Apostle Paul and Women in the Church* (Glendale, CA: Regal Books, Div. G/L Publications, 1977), 92, 138ff.
29. Scanzoni and Hardesty, *All We're Meant to Be*, 32.

CHAPTER FOUR *The Institution of Marriage*

1. Province of Alberta, Canada, statistics for 1984.
2. James B. Hurley, *Man and Woman in Biblical Perspective* (Grand Rapids: Zondervan Publishing House, 1981), 101.

3. *Ibid.*, 111.
4. Francis A. Schaeffer, *The Great Evangelical Disaster* (Westchester, IL: Crossway Books, 1984), 130.
5. *Ibid.*, 131.
6. Susan T. Foh, "What Is the Woman's Desire?," *Westminster Theological Journal*, 37 (Spring 1975): 382.
7. Hurley, *Man and Woman in Biblical Perspective*, 218-219.
8. Letha Scanzoni and Nancy Hardesty, *All We're Meant to Be* (Waco, TX: Word Books, 1974), 30.
9. E. Margaret Howe, *Women and Church Leadership* (Grand Rapids: Zondervan Publishing House, 1982), 139.
10. Don Williams, *The Apostle Paul and Women in the Church* (Glendale, CA: Regal Books, Div. G/L Publications, 1977), 139.
11. Howe, *Women and Church Leadership*, 55.
12. Scanzoni and Hardesty, *All We're Meant to Be*, 30.
13. Howe, *Women and Church Leadership*, 60.
14. Scanzoni and Hardesty, *All We're Meant to Be*, 107.
15. Virginia R. Mollenkott, *Women, Men and the Bible* (Nashville: Abingdon Press, 1977), 51.
16. Wayne Grudem, "Does *Kephale* ('head') Mean 'Source' or 'Authority Over' in Greek Literature? A Survey of 2,336 Examples," cited in *The Role Relationship of Men and Women*, George W. Knight III (Chicago: Moody Press, 1985), 53.
17. *Ibid.*, 56.
18. *Ibid.*, 58.
19. *Ibid.*, 60.
20. *Ibid.*, 80.
21. Kenneth O. Gangel, "Biblical Feminism and Church Leadership," *Bibliotheca Sacra*, January-March 1983, 56.
22. Hurley, *Man and Woman in Biblical Perspective*, 146-147.
23. Paul K. Jewett, *Man as Male and Female* (Grand Rapids: Wm. B. Eerdmans Publishing Co., 1975), 58-59.

CHAPTER FIVE *The Male Role in Marriage*

1. James Dobson, *What Wives Wish Their Husbands Knew About Women* (Wheaton, IL: Tyndale House, 1981), 67.
2. David W. Augsburger, *For Men Only*, ed. J. Allen Peterson (Wheaton, IL: Tyndale House, 1973), 54.
3. James B. Hurley, *Man and Woman in Biblical Perspective* (Grand Rapids: Zondervan Publishing House, 1981), 147-148.
4. *Ibid.*, 156.
5. Susan T. Foh, *Women and the Word of God* (Phillipsburg, NJ: Presbyterian and Reformed Publishing Co., 1979), 133.
6. George W. Knight III, *The New Testament Teaching on the Role Relationship of Men and Women* (Grand Rapids: Baker Book House, 1977), 35.
7. Hurley, *Man and Woman in Biblical Perspective*, 156.

CHAPTER SIX *The Female Role in Marriage*

1. George W. Knight III, *The New Testament Teaching on the Role Relationship of Men and Women* (Grand Rapids: Baker Book House, 1977), 13.

2. Francis A. Schaeffer, *The Great Evangelical Disaster* (Westchester, IL: Crossway Books, 1984), 135.

3. *Ibid.*, 136.

4. Susan T. Foh, *Women and the Word of God* (Phillipsburg, NJ: Presbyterian and Reformed Publishing Co., 1979), 130.

5. Andre S. Bustanoby, "Love, Honor and Obey," *Christianity Today*, June 1969, 13.

6. Genesis 12:14, 15; 1 Peter 3:5, 6.

7. Genesis 16:6.

8. Genesis 21:10ff.

CHAPTER SEVEN *Stereotypes*

1. The philosophy of feminism has perpetuated the fallacy that submission presupposes certain negative personality traits.

2. J. Robertson McQuilkin, *Understanding and Applying the Bible* (Chicago: Moody Press, 1983), 54.

3. James B. Hurley, *Man and Woman in Biblical Perspective* (Grand Rapids: Zondervan Publishing House, 1981), 222.

4. *Ibid.*

5. *Ibid.*

6. *Ibid.*, 223.

7. *Ibid.*

8. Zane C. Hodges, unpublished view of, as outlined by Dr. Bruce Waltke in letter to author, January 22, 1987.

9. Proverbs 1:8; 6:20; 10:1; 15:20; 17:25; 23:22.

10. Susan T. Foh, *Women and the Word of God* (Phillipsburg, NJ: Presbyterian and Reformed Publishing Co., 1979), 190.

11. *Ibid.*, 190. A book which builds a strong case for women remaining in the home is: Mary Pride, *The Way Home — Beyond Feminism, Back to Reality* (Westchester, IL: Crossway Books, 1985).

CHAPTER EIGHT *The Role of Women in the Church*

1. As quoted in Letha Scanzoni and Nancy Hardesty, *All We're Meant to Be* (Waco, TX: Word Books, 1974), 54.

2. E. Margaret Howe, *Women and Church Leadership* (Grand Rapids: Zondervan Publishing House, 1982), 136-159.

3. Brian D. Johnson, "A New Catholic Code," *Macleans Magazine*, February 1983, 41; Also: Brian D. Johnson, "A Church Divided," *Macleans Magazine*, January 1983, 29-38.

4. Susan T. Foh, *Women and the Word of God* (Phillipsburg, NJ: Presbyterian and Reformed Publishing Co., 1979), 98.

5. Charles C. Ryrie, *The Role of Women in the Church* (Chicago: Moody Press, 1958), 71-72.

CHAPTER NINE *Headship and Head Coverings*

1. Susan T. Foh, *Women and the Word of God* (Phillipsburg, NJ: Presbyterian and Reformed Publishing Co., 1979), 101.

2. Hans Conzelmann, *1 Corinthians* (Philadelphia, PA: Fortress Press, 1975),

185; Stephen B. Clark, *Man and Woman in Christ* (Ann Arbor, MI: Servant Books, 1980), 168-169.

3. Charles C. Ryrie, *The Role of Women in the Church* (Chicago: Moody Press, 1958), 72.

4. James B. Hurley, *Man and Woman in Biblical Perspective* (Grand Rapids: Zondervan Publishing House, 1981), 170; John Peter Lange, *Commentary on the Holy Scriptures*, Vol. 5, (Grand Rapids: Zondervan Publishing House, 1960), 224.

5. George W. Knight III, *The New Testament Teaching on the Role Relationship of Men and Women* (Grand Rapids: Baker Book House, 1977), 32.

6. Hurley, *Man and Woman in Biblical Perspective*, 167.

7. Lange, *Commentary on the Holy Scriptures*, 224; John Calvin, *New Testament Commentaries*, Vol. 1 (Grand Rapids: Wm. B. Eerdmans Publishing Co., 1972), 231.

8. E.W. Bullinger, *A Critical Lexicon and Concordance to the English and Greek New Testament* (Grand Rapids: Zondervan Publishing House, 1975), 193.

9. Gary Inrig, *Life in His Body* (Wheaton, IL: Harold Shaw Publishers, 1975), 164.

10. Foh, *Women and the Word of God*, 111.

11. Gordon David Thomas, "A Sign of Respect in Church Worship," Sermon Notes, March 13, 1983, Calvary Baptist Church, Edmonton, Alberta, Canada.

12. Ryrie, *The Role of Women in the Church*, 74.

13. Bullinger, *A Critical Lexicon*, 323.

14. Hurley, *Man and Woman in Biblical Perspective*, 206.

15. John F. MacArthur, *The MacArthur New Testament Commentary — 1 Corinthians* (Chicago: Moody Press, 1984), 259.

16. Inrig, *Life in His Body*, 167.

17. MacArthur, *New Testament Commentary*, 259.

18. *Ibid.*

19. Ephesians 3:9, 10.

20. Inrig, *Life in His Body*, 167.

21. Lange, *Commentary on the Holy Scriptures*, 228.

22. Inrig, *Life in His Body*, 167.

23. Lange, *Commentary on the Holy Scriptures*, 228.

24. Clark, *Man and Woman in Christ*, 181.

25. *Ibid.*

26. Letha Scanzoni and Nancy Hardesty, *All We're Meant to Be* (Waco, TX: Word Books, 1974), 65, 57; Virginia R. Mollenkott, *Women, Men and the Bible* (Nashville: Abingdon Press, 1977), 99; Don Williams, *The Apostle Paul and Women in the Church* (Glendale CA: Regal Books, Div. G/L Publications, 1977), 67; Dorothy R. Pape, *In Search of God's Ideal Woman* (Downers Grove, IL: InterVarsity Press, 1976), 126; E. Margaret Howe, *Women and Church Leadership* (Grand Rapids: Zondervan Publishing House, 1982), 59-60.

27. Clark, *Man and Woman in Christ*, 175-176.

28. Henry A. Virkler, *Hermeneutics: Principles and Processes of Biblical Interpretation* (Grand Rapids: Baker Book House), 227-229.

29. Inrig, *Life in His Body*, 166.

30. Walter L. Liefield, *New Testament Exposition* (Grand Rapids: Zondervan Publishing House, 1984), 145-146; MacArthur, *New Testament Commentary*,

256; Charles Hodge, *A Commentary on 1 & 2 Corinthians* (Worcester, Great Britain: Billing & Sons Ltd., 1983), 205

31. Pape, *In Search of God's Ideal Woman,* 126.
32. Bruce Waltke, "1 Corinthians 11:2-16: An Interpretation," *Bibliotheca Sacra* 135 (1978): 46-47; Foh, *Women and the Word of God,* 258; Inrig, *Life in His Body,* 171.

In addition to contextual considerations, historical precedent within the Christian community testifies to the cross cultural nature of the practice. (It is only in the past three or four decades that its observance has slipped away — particularly in Western society.) We may also wish to consider Virkler's fifth hermeneutical step: It is better to treat a command as cross-cultural and be over-scrupulous in our desire to obey God than to treat it as culture-bound and neglect a requirement of God. For these reasons, this author favors the second view.

CHAPTER TEN *Verbal Participation*

1. Letha Scanzoni and Nancy Hardesty, *All We're Meant to Be* (Waco, TX: Word Books, 1974), 68.
2. *Ibid.*, 69.
3. Dr. Nathaniel West, "Women and Church Ministry," pamphlet (Star Rt., Box 11, Alden, N.Y., n.d.), 20.
4. E.W. Bullinger, *A Critical Lexicon and Concordance to the English and Greek New Testament* (Grand Rapids: Zondervan Publishing House, 1975), 663.
5. Kenneth O. Gangel, "Biblical Feminism and Church Leadership," *Bibliotheca Sacra*, January-March 1983, 58.
6. Gary Inrig, *Life in His Body* (Wheaton, IL: Harold Shaw Publishers, 1975), 58.
7. West, "Women and Church Ministry," 19.
8. Don Williams, *The Apostle Paul and Women in the Church* (Glendale, CA: Regal Books, Div. G/L Publications, 1977), 70.
9. D.A. Carson, *Exegetical Fallacies* (Grand Rapids: Baker Book House, 1984), 131.
10. Stephen B. Clark, *Man and Woman in Christ* (Ann Arbor, MI: Servant Books, 1980), 207.
11. Matthew 28:8, 9.
12. Luke 1:18-20.
13. Clark, *Man and Woman in Christ*, 373-374.
14. *Ibid.*, 382.
15. *Ibid.*, 385.
16. See also: Eleonore Maccoby, *The Psychology of Sex Differences* (Stanford, CT: Stanford University Press, 1974).
17. Clark, *Man and Woman in Christ*, 204.
18. *Ibid.*, 695.
19. Genesis 3:6.
20. J. I. Packer, *Keep in Step with the Spirit* (Old Tappan, NJ: Fleming H. Revell Co., 1984), 215-217.
21. Susan T. Foh, *Women and the Word of God* (Phillipsburg, NJ: Presbyterian and Reformed Publishing Co., 1979), 119.
22. Charles C. Ryrie, *The Role of Women in the Church* (Chicago: Moody Press, 1958), 76.

23. George W. Knight III, *The New Testament Teaching on the Role Relationship of Men and Women* (Grand Rapids: Baker Book House, 1977), 45.
24. Ryrie, *The Role of Women in the Church*, 77.
25. Bullinger, *A Critical Lexicon*, 894.
26. Knight, *The New Testament Teaching*, 31; Kenneth O. Gangel, "Biblical Feminism and Church Leadership," *Bibliotheca Sacra*, January-March 1983, 61.
27. Williams, *The Apostle Paul and Women in the Church*, 111.
28. Scanzoni and Hardesty, *All We're Meant to Be*, 71.
29. *Ibid.*, 72.
30. Williams, *The Apostle Paul and Women in the Church*, 114.
31. Scanzoni and Hardesty, *All We're Meant to Be*, 72.
32. Foh, *Women and the Word of God*, 123-124.
33. *Ibid.*, 119.
34. James B. Hurley, *Man and Woman in Biblical Perspective* (Grand Rapids: Zondervan Publishing House, 1981), 196–197.
35. Dorothy R. Pape, *In Search of God's Ideal Woman* (Downers Grove, IL: InterVarsity Press, 1976), 146, 155, 177, 235.
36. Hurley, *Man and Woman in Biblical Perspective*, 200.
37. Pape, *In Search of God's Ideal Woman*, 149.
38. Titus 2:4.
39. Inrig, *Life in His Body*, 171-172.

CHAPTER ELEVEN *Offices for Women*

1. Laura Sabia, Interview on "The National," CTV Broadcasting Corporation, Canada, July 1985.
2. Dorothy Jongeward and Dru Scott, *Affirmative Action for Women* (Reading, MA: Addison-Wesley Publishing Co., 1975), 102–105.
3. *Ibid.*, 113.
4. *Ibid.*, 114.
5. James B. Hurley, *Man and Woman in Biblical Perspective* (Grand Rapids: Zondervan Publishing House, 1981), 200.
6. *Ibid.*, 201.
7. Stephen B. Clark, *Man and Woman in Christ* (Ann Arbor, MI: Servant Books, 1980), 197.
8. *Ibid.*, 200.
9. *Ibid.*, 196.
10. George W. Knight III, *The New Testament Teaching on the Role Relationship of Men and Women* (Grand Rapids: Baker Book House, 1977), 39.
11. Hurley, *Man and Woman in Biblical Perspective*, 233.
12. Knight, *The New Testament Teaching*, 39.
13. Susan T. Foh, *Women and the Word of God* (Phillipsburg, NJ: Presbyterian and Reformed Publishing Co., 1979), 93.
14. Hurley, *Man and Woman in Biblical Perspective*, 121.
15. Clark, *Man and Woman in Christ*, 131.
16. *Ibid.*, 230.
17. E. Margaret Howe, *Women and Church Leadership* (Grand Rapids: Zondervan Publishing House, 1982), 69, 82.
18. Francis A. Schaeffer, *The Great Evangelical Disaster* (Westchester, IL: Crossway Books, 1984), 146.

19. Clark, *Man and Woman in Christ*, 625.

20. *Ibid.*, 626.

21. Hurley, *Man and Woman in Biblical Perspective*, 230–231.

22. Robert M. Lewis, "The 'Women' of 1 Timothy 3:11," *Bibliotheca Sacra* 136 (January–March 1979): 168.

23. *Ibid.*, 170.

24. Letha Scanzoni and Nancy Hardesty, *All We're Meant to Be* (Waco, TX: Word Books, 1974), 62.

25. Lewis, "The 'Women' of 1 Timothy 3:11," 169.

26. *Ibid.*, 170.

27. Charles C. Ryrie, *The Role of Women in the Church* (Chicago: Moody Press, 1958), 85.

28. Kenneth O. Gangel, "Biblical Feminism and Church Leadership," *Bibliotheca Sacra*, January-March 1983, 61.

29. Knight, *The New Testament Teaching*, 51.

30. Gary Inrig, *Life in His Body* (Wheaton, IL: Harold Shaw Publishers, 1975), 116.

31. Hurley, *Man and Woman in Biblical Perspective*, 123.

32. Ryrie, *The Role of Women in the Church*, 89.

33. Gangel, "Biblical Feminism and Church Leadership," 61.

34. Foh, *Women and the Word of God*, 96; Gangel, "Biblical Feminism and Church Leadership," 62.

35. Clark, *Man and Woman in Christ*, 119–120.

36. Lewis, "The 'Women' of 1 Timothy 3:11," 171ff.

37. *Ibid.*, 173.

38. *Ibid.*

39. *Ibid.*, 175.

40. Foh, *Women and the Word of God*, 261.

41. Clark, *Man and Woman in Christ*, 57.

CHAPTER TWELVE *Feminism*

1. Elizabeth Schussler Fiorenza, *In Memory of Her* (New York: Crossroad Publishing Co., 1985), 52.

2. *Ibid.*, 11, 12.

3. Elizabeth Cady Stanton, *The Woman's Bible* (1898), as quoted by Fiorenza, *In Memory of Her*, 7.

4. Fiorenza, *In Memory of Her*, 32.

5. *Ibid.*, xxiv.

6. *Ibid.*, 41.

7. *Ibid.*, 18.

8. *Ibid.*

9. Carol Christ, "Why Women Need the Goddess: Phenomenological, Psychological and Political Reflections," in Carol Christ and Judith Plaskow, eds., *Womanspirit Rising: A Feminist Reader in Religion* (New York: Harper & Row, 1979), 273-287.

10. Naomi Goldenberg, *Changing of the Gods: Feminism and the End of Traditional Religions* (Boston: Beacon Press, 1979), 93–94.

11. A. Duane Litfin, "Evangelical Feminism: Why Traditionalists Reject It," *Bibliotheca Sacra* 136 (1979): 267.

12. Fiorenza, *In Memory of Her*, 33.
13. H. Wayne House, "Paul, Women and Contemporary Evangelical Feminism," *Bibliotheca Sacra* 136 (January-March 1979): 40.
14. Virginia R. Mollenkott, *Women, Men and the Bible* (Nashville: Abingdon Press, 1977), 95, 105; Dorothy R. Pape, *In Search of God's Ideal Woman* (Downers Grove, IL: InterVarsity Press, 1976), 182, 206.
15. Refer to R. C. Sproul, *Explaining Inerrancy: A Commentary* (Oakland, CA: International Council on Biblical Inerrancy, 1980).
16. Henry A. Virkler, *Principles and Processes of Biblical Interpretation* (Grand Rapids: Baker Book House, 1981), 31–32.
17. *Ibid.*, 32.
18. Bernard Ramm, *Protestant Biblical Interpretation* (Grand Rapids: Baker Book House, 1970), 138.
19. J. Robertson McQuilkin, *Understanding and Applying the Bible* (Chicago: Moody Press, 1983), 54.
20. *Ibid.*, 54; Ramm, *Protestant Biblical Interpretation*, 104.
21. Richard Mayhue, "Cutting it Straight," Part 4, *Moody Monthly* 85:4 (December 1984): 96.
22. Virkler, *Principles and Processes*, 226.
23. *Ibid.*, 227-230.
24. Mollenkott, *Women, Men and the Bible* (Nashville: Abingdon Press, 1977), 84.
25. Pape, *In Search of God's Ideal Woman*, 188–189.
26. Susan T. Foh, *Women and the Word of God* (Phillipsburg, NJ: Presbyterian and Reformed Publishing Co., 1979), 7.
27. Paul K. Jewett, *Man as Male and Female* (Grand Rapids: Wm. B. Eerdmans Publishing Co., 1975), 131.
28. Letha Scanzoni and Nancy Hardesty, *All We're Meant to Be* (Waco, TX: Word Books, 1974), 15.
29. Litfin, "Evangelical Feminism," 263.
30. William O. Walker, "1 Corinthians 11:2-6 and Paul's Views Regarding Women," *Journal of Biblical Literature* 94 (March 1975): 109.
31. House, "Paul, Women and Contemporary Evangelical Feminism," 47.
32. James B. Hurley, *Man and Woman in Biblical Perspective* (Grand Rapids: Zondervan Publishing House, 1981), 126.
33. *Ibid.*, 126.
34. Ben Witherington III, "Rite and Rights for Women — Galatians 3:28," *New Testament Studies* 27 (1978): 594.
35. *Ibid.*, 601–602.
36. Hurley, *Man and Woman in Biblical Perspective*, 127.
37. Jewett, *Man as Male and Female*, 145.
38. Krister Stendahl, *The Bible and the Role of Women*, trans. Emilie T. Sander (Philadelphia: Fortress Press, 1966), 32.
39. Mollenkott, *Women, Men and the Bible*, 103.
40. Litfin, "Evangelical Feminism," 261.
41. *Ibid.*, 266.
42. Francis A. Schaeffer, *The Great Evangelical Disaster* (Westchester, IL: Crossway Books, 1984), 138.

CHAPTER THIRTEEN *Towards a Concept of Ministry*

1. R. Paul Stevens, *Liberating the Laity* (Downers Grove, IL: InterVarsity Press, 1985), 21.
2. *Ibid.*, 21.
3. Hendrik Kraemer, *A Theology of the Laity* (London: Lutterworth Press, 1958), 51-52.
4. Stevens, *Liberating the Laity*, 21.
5. Jo Berry, *The Priscilla Principle* (Grand Rapids: Zondervan Publishing House, 1984), 102.
6. Romans 12:6ff; 1 Corinthians 12:4, 28-30.

SCRIPTURE INDEX

INDEX